LIVE
WITH YOURSELF
AND
LIKE IT

LIVE
WITH YOURSELF
AND
LIKE IT

On the Dangers of Being Serious

Colette Hovasse

Translated by Erika J. Papp

ORBIS BOOKS
MARYKNOLL, NEW YORK

Originally published in 1970 as
Du Danger d'etre Serieux
by Editions du Centurion, Paris

Copyright © 1972 Orbis Books, Maryknoll, New York 10545
Library of Congress Catalog Card Number 73-190116
Manufactured in the United States of America
Second printing

Contents

In memory of Anne Guillou, my goddaughter,
born to the True Life at age 22,
Wednesday of Holy Week, 1968

To Gerda Hegedus, whose
humor, friendship, courage and great talent
have helped me very much.

Introduction

While I am alone I am someone with no body at all, no position, no face. Only when someone comes . . . . It is only then that I exist.

Paul Claudel, *Le Pere humilie*

It's dangerous to be serious.

For whom is it dangerous to be serious? For other people, certainly, because we bore them—isn't laughter the distinguishing characteristic of man? But at the same time, there is the added risk that we shall make them feel guilty, to a slight or a greater degree, depending on their level of emotional maturity.

If an individual is of an imaginative nature, the very "relaxed" type, but is nevertheless rather lacking in self-confidence, won't he be made to feel guilty by those serious people for whom everything is seen in terms of Duty, Skill,

Profession—indeed, Vocation— Obligations, Principles (those sacrosanct principles which the Pharisees have handed down to us for painting whited sepulchers)? This regiment of capital letters which makes you a Good Man, a Perfect Mother—in other words, someone who is a success: a Model! These are formidable individuals who make you aware of your failings, because you feel that everything that you have is written in small letters—work, family, children, the search for that self-confidence which others, the fortunate people, seem to you to have.

But if you have any tendency toward self-depreciation, or discouragement, or depression —in other words, if you have a serious lack of self-confidence or have lost your self-confidence for the time being, the proximity of serious people is likely to aggravate your condition. The perfection which they wish to incarnate (they brandish their virtues like flame-throwers) inevitably increases your feelings of incompetence, helplessness, worthlessness—in short, of guilt. The only people secure in the company of paragons like these are individuals who are so fortunate as to have been endowed by their parents with solid good sense and self-confidence and by heaven with a sense of humor, precious gift that it is.

Does being serious contain dangers for oneself? Yes, indeed; for it is an attitude which reveals a lack of realism and of proportion, and hence an incapacity for seeing the funny side of things. Who does a person think he is, within the context of creation and society, when he hasn't the good sense to reflect upon himself with humility and simplicity, without exaggerating his qualities, his abilities and his importance?

Dangers for oneself? Assuredly. For being serious often means that we "take ourselves seriously," and that denotes a regrettable lack of humor. It also involves the danger that we shall isolate ourselves from others by placing ourselves above their criticism—and hence beyond their help. (And we cannot do anything on our own, especially not improve, know, or change ourselves.) There is the added danger that we shall be isolated from ourselves, for we shall no longer be seeing ourselves except through the role we believe ourselves obliged to play.

In the final analysis, isn't the danger of being serious really that we isolate ourselves, cut ourselves off from others and from everything which could assist us toward self-knowledge and self-improvement? We become blind with regard to ourselves, and every contradiction poses a threat to all our certainties—a situation full of real anguish.

Danger, yes; because this type of person is fundamentally destructive. He has lost (unless he never had it) all realism and all objectivity and hence is capable of the worst stupidities.

Why do we
Take Ourselves Seriously?

Because most of the time we can't help it

The fact is that we are led into it unconsciously, forced to play a role. This is something which cannot be repeated often enough to people who like to talk in a vague way about the inviolability of the Will. Since Freud, we know that the will is often held in bondage by forces much more powerful than itself, forces we are unable to resist until we have been made aware of our condition. This process of becoming aware is something more easily said than done, as all those who have courageously made the attempt can testify.

Claudine, on the verge of a severe mental depression, was isolated in an unfriendly city. She was visited by the only relations she had in the area, her brother and her sister-in-law, who, before their visit, had consulted a priest in whom they had implicit confidence. Here is the theme of their "sermon" to this forty-year-old woman on the brink of suicide:

My dear Claudine, your brother and I feel obliged to stop associating with you; you are a threat to the stability of our home. Your sense of values is completely warped. All you try to do is put on an act. But people ought to be sincerely what they are! We don't want the children—your nephews—exposed to this kind of attitude. You have a will! Do an about-face and start off again on the right foot. Go back to being the Claudine we love!

What superb psychology, this, and true Christian charity, too! A person in an agony of self-doubt is forced into an awareness of having made an even worse mess of her life than she supposed—seeing that she has become a danger to her family and her adored nephews, who are her only remaining joy in her state of depression. What an extraordinary feat of understanding on the part of the priest in the affair, who knew both parties well!

If Claudine did not commit suicide that day or in the days which followed, it was only because her knowledge of psychology enabled her to understand, even in her depressed condition, that the hypocritical attitude of her relations was quite unconscious: there were serious underlying problems which motivated the rejection on the part of one and the aggressivity of the other. So far as they knew, they were moved only by "good intentions."

Only charity could have made it possible for her to understand it and thus limit the damage it did to her; only charity could have given her the forebearance which helped her to pass it over in silence. But there she was, sunk in the depression which might have been warded off— perhaps—if she had been shown some understanding instead of being judged and told to "use her will power." As if a depressed person, who is in doubt of everything and himself most of all, were still capable of using any sort of will whatsoever for anything but his own self-destruction! Especially when his closest relations come to his assistance in such an effective manner.

We do what we can, and often enough it isn't much; but for the sake of ourselves and others we must obtain some insight into what it is that we are doing. Appealing to Claudine's will was the worst possible blunder, betraying a total incomprehension of a serious illness.

For one part of her family at this time, Claudine was "weak," and for the other, "shameful." What a help that was.

When will people learn that depression is first of all a doubting of self, an annihilation so total that the will, or what remains of it, can only be used toward the person's self-destruction in intensifying guilt, which is another way of committing suicide?

But depressed people are not alone in this plight. There are all those others whom a certain weakness makes liable to self-doubt, for one reason or another—they too are in danger of taking themselves seriously. They must be given confidence in themselves again by being shown love, friendship, unconditional affection, before they will be capable—on tiptoe, so to speak—of restoring the will to its proper place. One shudders at the thought that so many relatives go into action looking at the situation upside down!

Sophie exhibited a self-assurance that was quite excessive—it could have fooled only the blind. She lived it up, driving around in a sports car which provoked envy in several members of her family. When a depressive phase followed upon this euphoria (now it was easy to see the point of transition to ill health) she was plunged into a kind of hell. Her whole family united in shielding her; they joined forces to raise funds for her by selling the famous car. The relative entrusted with the affair congratulated her on what he considered a very good deal—she hadn't lost nearly as much as he had anticipated. What didn't enter his mind was that if the family had loaned her half that sum it would have tided her over. Probably she would have been able to pay it back in eighteen months without difficulty.

The self-assurance in her case was a symptom of ill health—it hid great despair, a profound self-doubt. This need to be noticed—it was all part of her effort to convince herself that she was not a total failure. But it was experienced by those around her as aggression. They wished (and told her so) that she would "face up" to the situation. And having done this they let her fall, leaving the recovery of her fortunes up to her own will power.

Is it possible to imagine a more mistaken kind of behavior? A greater lack of understanding? They dramatized everything, even the gravity of her financial deficit—calculating that it would take four years of great sacrifices for her to clear it up. (She did it, by herself, in two.)

They reproached her with her way of life, even getting down to the matter of her household linen. "From now on," they said, "you should be satisfied with a studio apartment and a small car. Besides, that is really more appropriate to your status." They were jealous of the well-appointed home she had made, of her domestic talents, and of the sports car.

Every time she tried to emerge from underwater, they pushed her head down again with the subtlest kind of cruelties ("You, who have never been able to keep your accounts straight . . . ."). In the guise of giving her aid and shelter, they visited on her a thousand and one allusions to the false scale of values which made her think of herself as someone with a "message"— instead of working out her salvation by thinking about her last end.

The reason a person puts on a front is that he is unable just to "be himself." Happy are those who are sufficiently well-balanced, at harmony with themselves, to be able simply to "be." But to hold it against others that they can't is hypocritical.

Who among us *has* never sinned, in some form or other—for indeed it is a sin, and may God preserve us from it—in this way.?

Don't we, for instance, cultivate the image of the "beaming mother of the family," while concealing a profound bitterness over being beset by material cares—a resentment sometimes discharged in sarcastic humor?

Don't we make a great pretense of being the "responsible father of the family" when as a matter of fact we break down in the face of the first big problem in the children's upbringing, refusing to consider the question in a constructive way and instead threatening to drop everything?

Aren't these ways of putting on a front much more hypocritical, and in a subtler way, than the sports car and the nice apartment?

Who amoung us can claim that he has never played a role?

Didn't the families of Claudine and Sophie play a role, that of self-styled Concerned Individuals, full of solicitude for these two whose faltering wills they would restore? They played the role of those in whom the will, frustrated most of the time, has developed by dint of activity: now they cannot do other than to adhere to the role of moralizer and redresser of wrongs within the family.

This is a subtle form of hypocrisy, but a role all the same: a way of *seeming* deliberately chosen, built up, elaborated. Claudine and Sophie, on the contrary, did what they could with what they had without pretending to set an example for anyone.

But the same axiom applies to these families as well: we do what we can with what we have, and sometimes that is not much. It can even be negative without a person's being to blame; he believes that he is acting with the best of intentions.

The role of the priest in Claudine's case is likewise involuntarily destructive. He too was taken in by Claudine's self-assurance, failing to glimpse, under it, an immense despair and the last flicker of a dynamism overwhelmed by failures and trials of all kinds. Instead of offering her a helping hand, which would have saved her, he sided with the "right-minded" people and threw the first stone! Sober responsibility combined with blindness, and infantile on the psychological level—all this prevents us from seeing that at every turn an excessive self-assurance is hiding a profound confusion that affects the vital fibers of the person's being and is often a compensation for a failure which could be traumatic for a very sensitive individual.

Those who take themselves seriously are forced to do so by a dangerous lack of self-confidence.

Isn't this paradoxical?

No, not if we are careful to explain our vocabulary.

It was Voltaire who said, in his *Essays on Morals*: "If men defined the words they use, there would be fewer disputes; and more than one kingdom has been overthrown by a misunderstanding."

The expressions "having confidence in oneself" and "having self-assurance" are often regarded as synonymous. Actually their meanings are, as we use them, exactly the opposite.

Having confidence in oneself is to know oneself and to accept oneself with one's faults as well as one's virtues; it is to have an accurate idea of one's worth. Oddly enough, confidence in oneself comes close to the Christian virtue of humility, which consists in a true knowledge of one's worth. In relation to God, not much of it remains ours; in relation to our fellow men, the positive balances out the negative most of the time. (That inspired educator Baden-Powell spoke of the five percent of good in the worst of individuals on the basis of which one can start to reconstruct the rest.)

Self-assurance, on the contrary, always betrays to the informed observer a lack of self-confidence; this inevitably involves the need of playing a role as a means of self-affirmation and self-assertion.

Taking ourself seriously means that we want to force others to recognize us as Someone Good, someone who has nothing to learn from anybody, since he knows everything better than everybody else—someone, therefore, who is entitled to esteem, to receive blind submission and obedience with no questions asked; someone who need regard neither criticism nor advice.

There are numerous examples of these unbearable people.

Frank, the shrewd founder of a business, the father of a family, authoritarian, aged seventy-five: he still intimidated his offspring in their fifties as well as his grandchildren; he never had real contact with anyone, nor was dialogue possible for him.

Within the business he had founded and developed with immense acumen he was the unchallenged master who quelled everyone with his eagle eye. He never missed a mistake—noticed the penny's difference in the accounts, the speck of dust on his desk.

His brilliant intellect laid down the law in the meetings of administrative boards over which he presided; his authority and the swiftness of his retorts silenced his colleagues, whom he made feel guilty and unimportant.

In the bosom of his family he terrorized his wife, his children, and his grandchildren. His home life had never been anything but a failure.

His wife had never meant more to him than

an object for the production of children to carry on his line, and after that an object of display owing to her elegance. All his home stood for was his social success. He had never listened to his wife nor really looked at her. It had not even struck him that she was a being capable of having ideas of her own; she was simply one of his possessions. Since, for the sake of peace, she had weakly allowed herself to be caught in this iron vise, they presented the appearance of a united couple, but all the children paid dearly for the fundamental misunderstanding between their parents in the latter's intimate relationships. All the homes which the children established were failures; of the six, three were divorced—the eldest, the one most deeply affected, three times.

Nevertheless, who would ever think that Frank himself had made a failure of his life? His immense social success, the lavish scale on which he entertained, misled everyone, especially himself.

It took a coronary thrombosis when he was seventy-five to penetrate his self-delusion. Facing death, he was brought to the realization that he was completely alone in a family whose members more or less consciously detested him and without exception feared him. His wife, he felt, longed for his death, which would free her, and perhaps, finally allow her to be herself.

At seventy-five he became aware, for the first time, that he had missed out on everything and that his life had been nothing but a sham, a role he had played to hide the truth from himself. He had never been capable of loving or, therefore, of receiving love. Raised by an austere, puritanical father, he had never developed any confidence in himself; he had built up that self-assured, patriarchal personality to compensate for this enormous lack in his affectivity. At the age of seventy-five—his father having been dead for thirty years—he was still seeking desperately, and unconsciously, to prove to his disapproving parent that he was not wholly worthless.

His sensitivity, mutilated by a rigid education, had shut itself off and he had developed, by way of compensation, an immense intelligence. The intellect then functioned, so to speak, in a vacuum, without the counterweight of the sensitivity which would have provided equilibrium. The result was obvious: nothing that he built up lasted; when he died the whole structure collapsed. Since he had never learned how to deal with people unless they were subservient and lacking in personality, he had refused to take his sons into the business; hence it did not survive him.

By the time that he had come to the realization of his mistakes, it was too late to repair the damage. His family could see him only in terms of the characteristics he had imposed upon himself throughout his lifetime. His efforts at dialogue met with incomprehension. The same was true with regard to his subordinates; he was unable to bring them out of their childish dependence on him.

This inability to divest himself of his role, to bring into the light of day a little scrap of sensitivity which was striving to come into being, killed him more surely than the coronary, from which he would have recovered.

But he died without his family's having any comprehension of the evolution which had taken place within him in the course of his last weeks. He had conditioned them too completely to himself as a personage; now it was impossible for them to see him as the person which, in the end, he wanted to be.

He died, condemned by his whole entourage to conform to an image until the end.

The essential thing for him was that he should be able, at last, to be an adult in facing and welcoming death.

A clergyman: tremendously busy, a brilliant preacher, a man of encyclopedic knowledge and profound faith, but quite incapable of teamwork and of keeping curates.

Sure of his knowledge in every field, and apparently quite devoid of humility, he had a tendency to center the Mass on the sermon he gave, rather than on the Eucharist. His parishioners couldn't help making a comparison between his personality and that of Nietzsche, on whom he preached to them throughout one whole Lent.

Unable to get along with his bishop, whose authority he did not accept, he ended up making himself hated by his parishioners: he had the church door shut in their faces at the beginning of the Entrance Hymn and compelled them to follow the Mass in a missal—of *his* choice. An all-around dictator, he discouraged all the parish enterprises and all his curates in succession, eventually keeping as followers (almost "fans") the sophisticated snobs and the least adult among his flock, whom he enthralled by his eloquence and his keen sense of the dramatic.

When the bishop finally removed him from the parish on twenty-four hours' notice, his supporters ceased, for the most part, to practice the faith "because Father X is not there any more." There was no longer any Mass possible for them in a city of 200,000 inhabitants.

The trouble here was a lack of emotional maturity in a painfully sensitive person who could not endure the slightest criticism or accept the smallest assistance.

At one and the same time a pastor, a curate, the moderator of every parish society, a social worker and juvenile judge, he legislated in accordance with his own affectivity, without taking the opinions of authorities or appeals to prudence into account.

His "exile"—which was what he felt it to be—plunged him into a severe depression, which followed on open insubordination.

After months of illness, he surfaced again, ripened, much more mature as the result of this trial.

Grace most evidently came to his assistance, enabling him to draw a lesson from his failure and to acquire a way of behaving that was more in keeping with his calling. But he remained very childish, very demanding, in his relations with others: his bishop realized this and gave him a solitary post with intellectual responsibilities.

Eric, a graduate *summa cum laude* of a poly-technic institute, was nevertheless incapable at the age of forty-five of assuming real responsi-bilities. A perpetual trainee, he went from one enterprise to another, interested by all the discoveries he made but rejecting the positions of authority for which he was qualified because the responsibilities they involved frightened him.

He was the father of a large family. The noise they made was too much for him, so he formed the habit of shutting himself up in his office, abdicating all his responsibility for their upbring-ing, which had to be assumed by his worn-out wife. Out of sight, out of mind: he neither really looked at his children nor listened to them, let alone establish any dialogue with them. So his wife struggled alone with her eight children—for he was really the first of this tribe.

A perpetual adolescent, he remained forever the student, never attaining to the emotional maturity which would have enabled him to be an adequate husband concerned for the health of his wife, a father and the head of a house-hold. He was incapable of assuming even a minimum of responsibility, whether with respect to his family, his work, or the tasks of a member of society. He was a bookworm and his mother's little boy—his wife continued to adore him under the perplexed gaze of his progeny.

All the children—four boys and three girls—presented problems: the boys were unable to develop their manhood because they did not have a father who was a man with whom to identify; the girls could not develop their femininity because their father did not "see" them and did not live as the man of the family, since the mother had been forced to assume the two roles. Inevitably, the girls became masculine, identifying themselves with their father in order to protect their mother because her husband was incapable of doing it.

This man of many parts—quite well-versed in any field of science or culture—remained Mother's little boy; on the emotional level, he had never advanced beyond the age of six. His wife, who had to play the role of second mother, had tremendous difficulties with her mother-in-law, who retained considerable authority over her little boy. Eric's self-assurance was quite a production. When he had the floor, no interruptions or contradictions were permitted. Totally lacking in humor, he was the all-around expert whose opinion was law.

How could he avoid taking himself seriously? It was the only means at his disposal for camouflaging the wreck of his life on the family level (where he was the laughingstock of his children) and the professional level (where no one took him seriously—"What a character!").

Eric did what he could with what he had: his childish affectivity and his university degree.

Jack, aged forty-five, was a reporter with an international reputation. He was always where the action was, whether in Vietnam or Memphis. His courage, love of adventure and cool head earned the respect of colleagues all over the world, and the sense of human values shown in his writing gained him a very special place with both editors and readers of a news service which covers the globe. He had an unerring sense of the role and influence of the press. In short, he was a journalistic hero.

But Jack's home life was a failure. He had a wife who loved him just as he was. She waited at home, fearing for him but never expressing her fear—she understood the appeal which this dangerous calling had for him.

He was shamelessly unfaithful to her; he was incapable of resisting the advances of women of any age. He often produced the most childish tangles of lies to account for his disappearances. Once, for instance, he had returned from an assignment in Vietnam and his wife was delighted at the prospect of celebrating their wedding anniversary together; it would be the first in five years when he had not been on the other side of the world. But the night before, he became involved with a seventeen-year-old who had asked him if his weekend were free. He went off to the country with her, leaving his wife in the midst of the preparations she had made for their anniversary.

This courageous man, "virile" though he was, had remained infantile in his sexuality. Incapable of control, he completely succumbed to his urges, ignoring his wife's love for the sake of an instant's pleasure. Although she saw through him, she knew that she was the only one he really loved. She took him for what he was, a child, and pretended to believe his lies, which were so transparent that they cut her to the heart. But she was crucified by his cheap affairs.

The time came when she could no longer camouflage these infidelities from her growing children—especially after the oldest, age eighteen, had met his father with one of his "friends" in a night spot frequented by young people.

Getting the children to take a tolerant attitude was a painful business for the mother, for they found her tolerance extremely difficult to understand, and they judged their father severely. All four were badly shaken up by his attitude and still more by the suffering they saw their mother endure. For that they could not forgive him.

Who would have expected to find such a mess in the family of a hero like this—the kind of man of action young people dream about? Ironic, considering the misery he brought to his own children.

Here again was a lack of emotional maturity due to an excessively strict upbringing in which even the mention of sex was taboo. Jack never matured in the area of sexuality, but remained on the level of a small child who cannot master and integrate his impulses. He could not "do otherwise"; it was "stronger than he." More clearly stated: "I am not the master of my subconscious; it manages me."

He too did what he could with what he had.

Lawrence, aged thirty-four, head of the legal

department of a big oil company. Married and the father of two small boys, aged four and three, he asked for a divorce from his wife, charging her with infidelity.

The social investigation in connection with the case and the testimony of witnesses showed that he had set a trap for his wife into which she, wholly unsuspecting, had fallen. Lawrence wanted custody of his children: his mother would raise them better.

The social inquiry revealed that this man, distinguished officer during the war and an excellent lawyer, was still six years old on the emotional level. His mother (she had a kind of museum exhibit of her little boy's first shoes, his first teddy bear, etc.) had kept him completely dependent on herself.

Lawrence took himself seriously. From his first visit to the office of the court's social assistant everything showed it: the assurance of his bearing, the briefcase containing his "file." No effort was spared to remind the social worker, in case she should forget it, that she would not be obliged to represent him on the legal level or in the sphere of child psychology.

His wife, who was charged with every sin in the book (incompetence, unworthy of being a mother, infidelity, inability to administer medical treatment), showed herself to be a well-balanced, sensible woman who had been gravely traumatized by a marriage which was sexually very abnormal.

She said that her husband was so much attached to his mother that he went to have coffee with her every day. When some friends had taken the young couple to the movies without inviting the mother-in-law to come along, they were asked to keep this excursion secret from her. The result of this abnormal attachment to his mother was impotence on the part of the husband which was total when she was in the vicinity. He was unconsciously unable "to cheat on his mother"—characteristic of the Oedipus complex. The only times he could have normal relations with his wife were when they were on vacation.

The social worker realized with alarm that the mother-son team had been long plotting this affair in order to rear the two children in the reconstituted "family," without the foreign element of the one who had brought them into the world.

Although the social inquiry found evidence against the father, he won the case in court after a long-drawn-out and ruthless fight full of unsavory elements. Custody of the children was given to the grandmother.

A year later the mother committed suicide.

It had been impossible for the social worker, in the course of a dozen hour-long conferences, to bring Lawrence to a more reasonable idea of his children's emotional needs: his mother-spouse seemed to him better equipped to preserve their emotional balance than their own mother. His Oedipus complex was so deeply rooted that every fact was an argument in favor of his position. It was on the basis of this total certitude that he had set himself the objective of keeping his children by hook or by crook.

He did what he could with what he had.

If playing a role and taking oneself seriously is more common among men—we shall see why later on—women are not immune to this illness, for illness it is.

Miss Durand, aged fifty, a doctor of laws, was the head of personnel in a large corporation. She was very competent in her job, which she had been doing for twenty years, being a top expert in its legal aspects. Authoritative, masculine, dictatorial. She had made herself feared by the entire staff, her superiors included. They kept on good terms with her by letting her alone, instead of attempting to undo some of the damage she caused.

She was absolutely typical of the inhibited old maid. She avenged her spinsterhood and her lack of fulfillment by bullying those who had the misfortune to displease her—and sometimes she did not even know them except through their files. For example, she refused a promotion to a file clerk whose only offense had been to win a contest. Miss Durand had, as a consequence, seen her being interviewed on television.

She blocked the advancement of another girl because she was pretty and highly regarded (the written recommendations in her file praised her femininity and diplomacy). She "lost" the file of a third girl who had not taken her seriously enough.

This poor woman, a kind of general on a small scale, was the victim of her physical unattractiveness, her involuntary celibacy, and her profession: hers was a prestigious job which also gave her an excellent opportunity of exercising her sadism on weaker persons.

Unfortunately, everyone is familiar with the type of the aging nurse who is conscientious, masculine, with the suggestion of a moustache. She is the terror of the establishment—doctors as well as patients are in awe of her; yet her heart melts at the sight of a hungry stray cat on which she will lavish the attention and gentleness which the patients long to see manifested in their regard.

These poor women are maimed in their sensitivity. Very often it has shut itself off, owing to an exposure to suffering which was too early and too unmitigated; unable to integrate the experience or come to terms with it, they could only armor their sensitivity against it. Now they are incapable of manifesting this sensitivity toward human beings; only the most pitiful of animals can find the way to their hearts.

Under their dictatorial manner they too lack confidence in themselves. They are forced to play this role in order to shelter their sensitivity, doubtless severely traumatized in their childhood. As a result they have been unable to integrate the suffering to which they have ministered all their lives.

They are completely lacking in self-confidence because they are unmarried and have never been capable of being loved. They have armored themselves and asserted themselves in order to conceal their distress and give an impression of dignity. They are capable of receiving love only from animals, in relation to which they can let down their guard. To explain this to those around them who have to endure their behavior would be bound to raise a laugh, but it should be taken into account all the same.

There was Micheline, the mother of a family, very sure of herself. One was put off at once by her aggressive lack of any makeup—whether a rejection of femininity was involved or a misdirected effort to be completely natural was not clear. Everything about her was contrived: the play of the eyelashes over the washed-out blue eyes—doubtless she had established her "type" around this feature—the very affected gestures of the hands, the tone of voice which was an effort to sound artless and naive.

She was extremely self-assured and apparently quite satisfied with her role. No one better equipped than she, she thought, to give her two children (the ideal number, in her opinion) a complete, well-thought-out and balanced rearing. Well-thought-out it was, one had to admit; but that it would be durable one could well doubt.

In line with her views on childrearing, she refused to give them any sex education. After all, she pointed out, they lived in the country; they would see the cows and the bulls. When someone expressed astonishment that she should compare the love her husband bore her with that of a bull for a cow, she scarcely reacted. Apparently she was frigid herself, and she couldn't bear to have "these things" mentioned before these dear little ones she was "preparing for life." When an unmarried psychologist with whom she had been induced to discuss her children tried to make her understand that it is really quite simple to approach this subject which she regarded as taboo, she retorted: "You don't know anything about it! If you were a married woman you would see how much more difficult it is than you think." And with that the subject was shelved with total finality. Looking down from her status as a married woman—and evidently finding marriage disappointing—she judged everything, decided everything intellectually, her sensitivity not entering in.

She was leaving out an essential part of her children's emotional education. One might ask whether it would be possible for her to do otherwise, and it would seem not. She too did what she could with what she had. Her frigidity blocked her from attributing any value to "those things," which she suppressed by denying. Wasn't this her way—and one of the only ways at her disposal—of finding her own equilibrium in the midst of disequilibrium?

Could one judge her? Criticize her? She was pitiable, and it would be difficult to help her unless she sought help. How could one reach the cause of this frigidity which conditioned her whole behavior and doubtless had its motivation in her early childhood? She would inevitably make her children ill in the affective sphere. This is the genesis of all familial neuroses, a kind of illness more hereditary than most others, which is transmitted in this way from one generation to another of neurotics.

Then there was that social worker—whose species is, thank heaven, beginning to die out. A hard-bitten spinster, very self-assured, taking full responsibility for "her" families. Having heard three lectures on Carl Rogers, she considered herself an expert in psychology. So she held "conferences" somewhat at random with clients who came to her, say, for information about going to a holiday camp (which she did not give), or did "therapy" with the illiterate convict who was anxious only to get a job when he was released.

She decided everything in "her" families: conjugal problems—her decision was against "family planning"—child guidance, budgetary matters; all, of course, in terms of her personal convictions. Needless to say, she was resented by families with a strong sense of personal liberty and passively endured by those who should have been encouraged to manage their own affairs.

Could she behave otherwise? An aggressive feminist, she was regarded as intolerable by men. They were rather afraid of her, too, because she set herself up as a competitor and didn't acknowledge any difference between herself and them. An unwilling spinster, she had to suppress a sensitivity badly mutilated by a domineering mother—and she compensated for it by taking herself seriously.

She too did what she could with what she had.

There was Josephine, who thought of herself as a born educator. She wanted to impose her ideas on all her married brothers and sisters, whom she regarded as a disgrace. All her neighbors found her intolerable because she tried to force her views on them too. She had "improved" the catechetical material which she taught their children; she never stopped preaching to them, in season and out of season, with regard to what they ought to give their children in order to prepare them for their last end—the only goal of education. She presented herself as a model mother because she was, as she put it, "intuitive" and "sure of her vocation." Meanwhile her own family was far from being a success.

Her oldest daughter, thirteen, was impossible. She was feared by her teachers and by all her cousins, to whom, following her mother's example, she wanted to lay down the law. She was incapable of adapting herself to any discipline whatsoever. Nevertheless all her mother saw in her was a future mother abbess!

Her son, shamelessly spoiled, was unpopular among his cousins, for no matter what happened, she alway decided in his favor against them. It was constantly emphasized that he had "all it takes to make a saint"; he took advantage of this by doing whatever he pleased.

She regarded her youngest daughter with far less favor; in fact, she treated her with a severity bordering on the ferocious because "that hussy" (aged three) dared to offer resistance to her mother.

She had quite literally domesticated her husband, though he had seemed to have personality enough before marrying her. She caused him to lose several jobs in succession by her intrigues, in which she engaged owing to her intuition and her vocation of being responsible for the salvation of others. People avoided her—they got out of her way!

Could she behave otherwise? Ruined by the hypocritical upbringing of parents centered entirely on themselves and the conventions, this poor girl discovered for herself—happily too late!—the vocation of a theologian in skirts to compensate for the authoritarian bullying she had had to endure. She built up a role for herself because she was not taught to love herself.

Finally there was Antoinette, a personnel director, who, at the age of forty, did a courageous about-face and changed the course of her life and of her career completely. She demonstrated a wonderful spirit of adaptation in bringing her situation under control and starting again.

Flattered by her friends by way of reassurance, because they were afraid of what her possibilities might be otherwise, Antoinette had become completely artificial. She took herself seriously to the point of infallibility; in her own mind she was a top expert in her profession. She had trouble in accepting her age, and under the pretext that she had to see a great many young people in connection with her job she wore mini-skirts, having bought them at a shop patronized by all the young people in town. The effect was rather ridiculous, but she was so preoccupied with the need to make herself feel younger (no doubt in order to suppress the years during which she had failed to get her bearings) as to be quite insensitive in this area.

She decided the future of everyone around her, with a pretension to psychological expertise which was only equaled by her maladroitness. When one of her friends was emerging painfully from a nervous depression she in effect closed the door again by declaring to her that the new job to which she was trying to make an adjustment was her "last chance." These two words, as ill-chosen as they were pretentious—what possible authority could she base herself on?—pursued the unfortunate young woman for six months, until the relapse occurred to which they contributed.

But Antoinette had become an oracle in her own eyes. Those who were not part of her circle of admirers found her difficult to tolerate. However, she was deaf to anything they might say, her whole concentration being on making herself clear.

Doesn't it seem evident that she had to put on blinkers and take herself seriously in order to erase the time she had lost? Could she have done otherwise? Perhaps, if her friends had not anchored her in her error by their flattery. One might ask what her problems with her father had been—apparently it was his attitudes that she was trying to imitate, even as she cultivated the image of a femininity much younger than her age which brought her essential balance into question.

Let us conclude this review with a look at that frieze on which Joseph Folliet has depicted types of these "right-minded" people with truculent brush strokes. These are Christians coming from Mass:

You are coming out of Mass, my brothers in Jesus Christ, and you are scattered around on the church steps and the sidewalk. Looking at you, I think of Friedrich Nietzsche growling into his bushy moustache: "I would believe in their salvation if they had more of an air of being saved." Frankly, except for a few of you, you don't look like witnesses of salvation and joy. Like everyone else—like the rest of the world, in fact—you look like the Knights of the Long Face. Here you are, coming from the Eucharist, from the joyous sharing of grace; yet you are not of a mind to sing Alleluia.

On the solemn people of the world:

And you, the solemn people I meet on the transcontinental railways and the transoceanic planes—executives with polished briefcases diplomats, international officials, politicians, journalists on the move, high-class swindlers —are you happy? Your walk, your facial expression, suggest that you are plagued by ulcers, that nervous depression or heart attacks are in the offing as the result of your melancholy.

Madame, your makeup, your vivacity, your chatter—none of it can hide the unhappiness which is preying on you. You don't know what joy is.

Then there is the matter of humor. Let's talk about our new breed of priests.

A friend of mine said to me: "These new priests—I find them altruistic, zealous, but . . . they aren't funny." What an odd criticism! But he went on to explain himself. "These priests are serious—in fact, they're too serious, they're solemn. They have no gaiety or humor. They don't make you want to be priests, like them." A wrong impression? I'm afraid not. Many young priests whom I like and admire would answer to this description. In fairness I must say that it would also apply to some older priests, longer in the priesthood. I sometimes miss the clergy of my youth with their noisy outbursts of Rabelaisian laughter. That earthy clerical laughter, which could offend no one but a hypocrite, was the expression of purity of heart and a youthful spirit.

No, my brothers in Christ and in the Church, you are not living to the full, and neither are your priests. Wrought upon by tensions and contentions, there is no repose nor refreshment in you. Men of the right, left or center, you all have a kind of bitter and hard solemnity which is the mark of the totalitarian. You are incredibly lacking in humor, seeming to be quite unaware that insofar as it involves, so to speak, standing off from oneself and gazing at oneself in detachment it is the first stage of humility—a virtue for which you haven't much regard anyway. If you do not diffuse joy, it is because the loveliest woman in the world can only give what she has. You ooze sadness, and time and again boredom. Brothers, smile![1]

To turn to the file on the clergy: here is the famous sermon of the bishop of Mainz as reported by Goethe.

He who feels his mind becoming cloudy at the third or fourth tankard of wine, to the extent that failing to recognize his wife, children and friends, he ill-uses them, should confine himself to two tankards if he does not wish to offend God and be minunderstood by his neighbor; but he who, having drunk four, five or six tankards, still remains capable of doing his work and keeping the commandments of his ecclesiastical and secular superiors may humbly and thankfully enter upon the portion that God has permitted him to take. May he nevertheless refrain from exceeding the limit of six measures, for it is rare that the infinite goodness of the Lord accords one of His children the favor which He has willed to accord to me, his unworthy servant. I drink eight tankards of wine a day, and no one can say that he has ever seen me yield to unjust anger or do injury to my relations or those of my acquaintance. May each of you, my brothers, fortify himself in the body and make merry in the spirit with the quantity of wine which the divine goodness has willed to allow him to absorb. Amen.

I am reminded of a parish priest who for a long time was the town's only subscriber to a rather sensational journal. "It amuses me be-

cause it is frightfully anticlerical," he explained.
"I learn a lot from it."

Why does a person lack confidence in himself?

Isn't it essentially because he has not reached
a full emotional maturity, which can only be the
product of a firm and harmonious rearing, beginning with the first months of life?

The foundations for emotional maturity are
laid very early in life. Indeed, if parents realize
its true importance, they are going to begin to
prepare this substructure even before they are
formally engaged—when they first discuss the
number of children they would like to have,
compare views and reach agreement as to the
kind of upbringing they will be given, they are
putting the first stones in place.

They will add to the structure in demonstrating a responsible fatherhood and motherhood by
bringing a child into the world when they know
they are capable of rearing him—that is, they are
sufficiently mature to behave in an adult way
toward him and independent enough financially
to provide for his needs. It is also desirable that
the mother should be prepared to devote herself
to the child completely during the first two
years of his life, giving up a job if need be in
order to give him all the attention he requires if
he is to develop harmoniously without the jolt-
ing experiences which are traumatic in their effects. The most important of psychological vita-
mins is tenderness.

A delivery facilitated by courses in painless childbirth will enable the infant to come in a gentler fashion into this world, so distressing with all its aggressions: the contact with air, noise, light; separation from his mother; the loss of her protective womb with its constant warmth; the loss, too, of her rhythmic heartbeat which has lulled him into security for nine months—security of which he must be made conscious from the moment of birth.

The infant is reassured by close contact with his mother, the warmth of her body and the rhythm of her heartbeat, which he hears again at every feeding-time. His bath water restores the comfortable aquatic environment of his lost paradise.

Another traumatizing stage is reached at weaning time. If this is done gradually and very gently, with an understanding of his anguish demonstrated by tender reassurance, another important foundation stone will have been laid. Allowing him to experience the novelty of a variety of tasty foods will help him not to feel attacked, and hence distressed, by anything that is new to him. It means beginning to develop in him a spirit of curiosity and a capacity for adaptation which are the most precious gifts we can give those who are going to be adults around 1990 and will have to live in a civilization of which we cannot form any real idea.

Attracted by what is new, curious to explore it and find out what it is, the child will be in control of himself and less inclined to suffer acutely from that distress, common and more or less normal, which we all feel in the face of a new situation. He will be in the best position to adapt himself to the new and derive the maximum benefit from it.

That is an important stone in the structure we are building.

Francis was a boy whom family circumstances prevented form continuing his schooling until graduation. Unable to get his bearings in life, he could do nothing but enlist in the army. At the age of thirty he returned to civilian life and began to look for a job.

Although his intelligence was no more than average, he succeeded in getting very high scores in all the tests administered to trainees in various enterprises, and five years later he found himself general manager of an important concern.

Why did he succeed where young men who were graduates of business colleges failed?

He was calm, he seemed to be perfectly balanced, he was full of driving energy and interested in everything new. He took the tests in a relaxed state, not in the least concerned by the fact that his job depended on them; so he scored higher than other applicants who were distressed, fearful—or too sure of themselves.

The tests did not lie. In spite of his lack of higher education, he had the intellectual curiosity and capacity for adaptation which enabled him to acquire an education—highly specialized, of course—for his career. His emotional balance ensured good relations with his subordinates; he did not try to lord it over them but was able to be receptive, listening attentively to their suggestions.

Around the age of two, at the time of toilet training, the child is going to add another important stone to the foundation of his affectivity. In learning to control himself, to make an effort to please his mother, he will be developing both his will power and his sense of altruism. It is for love of his mother that the small child will learn to use his potty-chair. It is an effort exacting an attention from him which mobilizes all his faculties. You see him, red-faced as a little rooster, concentrated on forcing his sphincter muscles, before it has become a conditioned reflex for him.

He is straining every nerve with the desire to please the one he loves—she who is his universe, his security, with whom it is necessary for him to be, and to remain, in harmony. The delight which she shows on seeing him master this technique repays him for all his efforts and teaches him the joy of giving. That is a considerable acquisition, a factor in his emotional balance, a joy which is essentially a part of his social life, and hence of his happiness.

Next comes the birth of a brother or sister, which will teach him that the love shown him by his mother can be shared without being diminished. It is important for the marriage he will enter into later, or even for his friendships and his social life, that he should not be exclusive and jealous in his affection. Isn't it essential to make, and integrate, the discovery that love has many forms and that several of its aspects can coexist in our heart without hindering one another? Once again it is his sense of altruism which is developing and being refined. This is an apprenticeship to the love which must be the primary objective of all education. Aren't we on earth to love? and be loved? The two go together. In order to know how to love and to be loved, one must have been valued, recognized as lovable, "able to be loved," from one's infancy. If his mother's unconditional love is that psychological vitamin which the tiny child's affectivity absorbs like a sponge, the child on his side must learn to respond to this love. He does it by his first smile and his first gift, which is the stool in his potty. It may seem paradoxical that such a discovery—the first grasp of the principle of oblation—should be occasioned by such an ill-smelling event. But that is the way it is.

This possibility of giving love is something of which the child is going to have harsh experience throughout the course of that very trying oedipal phase of its development. It is necessary, in effect, for the child to find its place in the family triangle, to discover intellectually and integrate emotionally the fact that it cannot be the husband of its beloved mother, or the wife of its adored father, but must find a husband like Papa, or a wife like Mamma, when it is ready to enter into marriage.

This is a very painful ordeal, one whose effects Sophocles analyzed with so much insight that Freud was able to use the name of Oedipus for it. A painful ordeal it certainly is to undo this knot, to emerge from the Father-Mother duality in order to turn toward the external world. The process will be very much facilitated by the harmonious union of the parents, which will enable the child to "integrate" much more easily the fact—which he experiences as cruel— that he cannot separate them and supplant the one he regards as a rival.

It is getting through this stage harmoniously which will enable the child later on to turn toward another of the opposite sex (it is at this age that homosexuals are made), to love this other in an oblative way and to form with him or her a new couple, completely independent and detached from the marriage of the parents. It is at this early age, between three and six, that the possibility develops of "leaving father and mother" in spirit and in truth, as the Gospel enjoins.

The possibility of establishing a harmonious couple demands that the young adult shall be in equilibrium on the level of sexuality—that is to say, the young man is totally ready to assume his masculinity and the young woman is feminine in all her tastes and aspirations and in her behavior. The oedipal phase would seem to us to be an essential stage in the building up of emotional maturity, since it completely conditions sexual equilibrium, which is the source of emotional equilibrium and hence of maturity in this same sphere.

We all know those big, burly men—longshoremen, perhaps, or wrestler-types—who conduct themselves like pet dogs in relation to their wives or as babies in relation to their mothers. They are stuck at that emotional age and are in a cramped position, tied up in knots, paralyzed so far as developing greater maturity in themselves is concerned.

When some of the stones are missing in the foundation, the building is dangerously lacking in solidity. When a section of a wall has been left out, a draft is let into the house, and nothing one can do will make it comfortable.

Isn't the problem the same for the child whom misunderstanding parents—the possessive love of his mother or the austerity of his father —have prevented from untangling this complex? For complex it is—that is to say, an emotional knot which results in the paralysis of a whole section of one's affectivity, a kind of scar on the unconscious which leads to an atrophy of the affectivity (lack of virility or femininity) or to a deformation of it (homosexuality). How is emotional maturity to be built up on such a shaky foundation? Of course, some people succeed— and there are many saints to prove it. In the final analysis, doesn't everything depend on grace? But at what cost in terms of human effort and human suffering!

How different it is when a child passes through this stage peacefully, making a positive adjustment which is productive of harmony within himself, since he is at ease with his sexuality. He is able to turn outwards and make a successful beginning of his schooling—in other words, he is able to enter society. In fact it is the discovery of society—its demands, its laws, its joys—which makes him ready for school.

Now comes a time of requirements and of discipline, a change in the emotional climate. The teacher will not be won over by a smile or a kiss; she insists on the line of writing she asked for. The collective life imposes limits, but it also brings an enrichment of play through companionship, with its own laws and rules, and then the choosing of personal friends. All these are the positive gains in this painful separation from his mother which also involves a change in schedule and a need of keeping pace with a collective life which are very tiring when one has been in the habit of playing alone, peacefully.

This stage will bring greater rewards if it is made easier for the child by expressions of affection and understanding. "How I missed you, darling!" Shouldn't this remark, addressed to a child returning home from school, be printed in the first pages of the manual of "words one must know how to say"? Whereas "Back to school at last! What a blessing! Now I'll have some peace" definitely belongs in the category of remarks to be avoided.

This stage will be even more profitable to the child if the parent is able to recognize the fatigue which the days at school bring on and lets the child "find himself" again in solitude. Indeed it is at this age that a person either keeps or loses the capacity to recover from fatigue and renew himself in silence and solitude. The child is spontaneously attuned to silence. One has only to watch him playing peacefully in his room or in a corner of the dining room, where he has managed to invent a universe for himself into which no one else enters; he can isolate himself in the midst of noise, though plainly it is more painful and difficult than in a room by himself. If we force him to be always at our side, sharing our occupations, our babble or the noise of the transistor, shall we not make him lose his precious capacity for withdrawing into solitude and silence and loving them?

Why does the peaceful, silent child become the adult for whom the transistor has become the indispensable complement rather than the companion? Does it really engage his attention? No, he submits to it because silence makes him apprehensive and all solitude frightens him.

Why, then, should we be surprised that he lives wholly on the surface of his own being, and so readily succumbs to the alienation which afflicts our civilization of consumers? Hasn't he lost an essential source of interior equilibrium and self-knowledge, and thus the capacity for accepting emotional maturity?

After the discovery of society, the child is still confronted with the necessity of emerging from himself to become a man. It is during the course of this painful stage of adolescence that he is going to lose the balance and harmony of the small child in order to build up the structure of the man he is going to be.

This period stretches out for long years, during which he will undergo much change—rather the way the caterpillar loses its beauty during the chrysalis phase in order to produce the elegant butterfly with dappled wings which will soar into the freedom of the sky.

It is a painful time of transition, and our civilization tends to prolong it by adding to the years of schooling and thus delaying, for great numbers of young people, the possibility of an independent life, the capacity for becoming self-supporting, establishing a home of their own, and finally assuming their full responsibilities.

It is in the course of this period, difficult for the parents but even more painful for the adolescent, that the young person, torn between the desire to regulate his own freedom with all its attendant responsibilities on the one hand, and the need for security written on the heart of every child, on the other, goes from one extreme to the other: liberty—protection; rejection of protection—liberty; anguish—protection once more. The instability of his behavior is equaled only by the anguish which this instability, which he is quite unable to comprehend, brings him.

Firm parents who give him the security deriving from their comprehending authority will help him to modify the deviations in his behavior with a view to attaining a new stability, very different from that of the child. In order to accomplish this he will have to reject the whole "culture" of the parental milieu which he has absorbed like a sponge; he will have to rethink everything—or try to—in order to make new choices with respect to his tastes, his vocation, his orientation toward life, his faith, independent of the influence of others.

This state of chronic opposition in which our adolescents live, so painful an experience for us, is as necessary to the development of their personality as was their docility when they were small children—as necessary as the first "No" of the two- or three-year-old tot which so hurt the feelings of his mother.

Won't knowing all this help us to accept the situation and live with it with less distress? Won't it help us to exercise the kind of liberal authority which adolescents need in order to regain the security which will enable them to pass through this final stage on the way toward emotional maturity? It is in the course of this period that they will learn how to regulate their own freedom and to assume the responsibilities which it implies on the personal, conjugal, family, professional, social, and civic level. They must learn to know themselves well, in order to accept themselves as they are, with their virtues and their defects—the former enabling them to bear with, and to reduce, the latter.

We should recall, in this connection, the remark of Baden-Powell which we quoted earlier about the five percent of good in the worst of persons on which we should build to eliminate the negative ninety-five percent.

Only a realistic self-knowledge in which strengths and weaknesses are included—what one can do and what one can't—will make possible a happy orientation to life, with respect to both society and oneself; only this will enable us to live harmoniously, without too many hard knocks.

To the extent that a person knows himself intellectually and accepts himself emotionally, he will be able to welcome suggestions, criticisms, and even setbacks, drawing out of each situation what is of positive value and thus rising above it.

It is to the extent that we lack this essential element of emotional maturity that we take ourselves seriously, play a role in order to impose on others the idea of ourselves which we so desperately need that they should have if we are to have the smallest amount of faith in ourselves.

Frank, Eric, the priest, Lawrence, Jack, and the rest—weren't they bound by the role they were forced to adopt as a means of camouflaging for themselves their lack of maturity and the failure of their emotional life? They had to play their role lest they perish—that was really what it was all about.

Their whole equilibrium was at stake. It was an off-center equilibrium, of course—balance in the context of unbalance—but it was all they were able to construct in order to survive. One had his Oedipus complex, another her lack of femininity, this one her spinsterhood and that one the suffering experience at too close quarters.

This role is like a plaster cast holding their weakened affectivity together. Taking themselves seriously serves these people as a crutch. They are psychological accident-victims. When shall we understand this? When will they be pitied instead of judged, so that a beginning may be made toward helping them? We shall see how later on.

The extreme limit of the demands which these troubled people make on us is represented by the mythomaniac, whose role can be summed up as "I speak, therefore I am." What I have said is what *is*. But we are required to believe the speaker, because his words assure him of his own reality only when their consistency is tested on the credence of another. In other words, there must be an echo.

Imagine, then, a mythomaniac in the last stages. He will be a person who is constantly throwing out lies in every direction, waiting for that echo which others will send back to him by believing what he says. No belief, no echo; no echo, no reality.

Then he will panic and keep sending out new lies until some send back their reassurance. But he never achieves anything. The slightest default on the part of others—the first suggestion that a credibility gap exists—and the man is shaken to his foundations. So the gap must be filled up fast with a new lie, and this too will collapse, perhaps in a month, or in an hour, or in the moment it is offered.

What this all adds up to is a kind of harlequin made up of bits and pieces in constant motion, a man-kaleidoscope in which past and future vanish in a present which is continually threatened.

It is this behavior, an aberration in the eyes of the layman but very upsetting for anyone who understands the fragility and the vulnerability of the person exhibiting it, which Alain Robbe-Grillet has described to some extent in his film *The Man Who Lies*. This film by the scenarist of *The Last Year at Marienbad* produces in a very striking way the image of a man forced to create a role for himself in order to survive—and to reconstruct it moment by moment because he is aware that it is breaking up and is going to leave him naked, totally exposed to every danger and every judgment.

This case, which is really pathological, is no more than a caricature of all those whom we have seen taking themselves seriously; basically they are driven, with the same helplessness, by the same motivating forces.

But why, then, does a person take himself seriously?

Why are all these unfortunates inexorably compelled to delude themselves and to give others the image they want to see reflected back to them?

Isn't it because they are lonely?

A person takes himself seriously because he is lonely

Frank, Eric, Jack, Miss Durand, Micheline and Josephine—weren't they lonely? Weren't our priest and our social worker lonely?

The married ones—wasn't it only the appearance of a couple which they presented with their partners? Were they capable of loving?

With their sensitivity frozen at an infantile level for various reasons, unable to accept themselves as men, as husbands, as fathers, or to accept their single state or their sexuality, or to engage in teamwork with their assistants—weren't they frightfully alone?

Wasn't Miss Durand alone—feeling that she must destroy those whom she felt to be rivals or who threatened the authority which she wanted to be total? Didn't she feel herself to be constantly under attack because she had forged an intellectual success to compensate for the mutilation of her sensitivity?

Wasn't Jack alone—intoxicated by the danger he sought all over the world but incapable of accepting his wife as a partner in marriage, or responding like an adult to the love she bore him?

Wasn't Lawrence alone—driving his wife to suicide in order to form a couple with his mother in accordance with the hangup he had had since the age of three? Will he be able to love his children in an oblative way? What image will he give them to identify themselves with? That of a man balanced in his manhood or that of a little boy twisted by an Oedipus complex?

Wasn't Eric alone—taking refuge behind his books, cut off from his wife and from the children whom he was only too capable of bringing into the world in large numbers? Did he know how to love them? or did he love himself?

Wasn't Frank alone, at the point of death, in the midst of a family with whom he had no real emotional tie?

Wasn't our priest alone, too, despite his fans —people who were still adolescents in the domain of faith? Incapable of teamwork, he was forced by his unconscious and the role he "had to" play to tyrannize everyone around him, including his parishioners.

Isn't the incapability of loving or being loved, because one is lacking in self-confidence and always on one's guard, at once a sign and an obvious cause of emotional immaturity? Nevertheless some of these people had built up an apparent social success, more or less deceptive depending on the individual but undeniable in the cases of Frank, Jack and Miss Durand, for instance. This is consoling evidence that one may lack emotional maturity in certain areas of one's personality and affectivity and yet be other than a failure. The thrust of vitality is there to help us reconstruct an equilibrium in the midst of disequilibrium.

Indeed this emotional isolation on the part of Frank, Eric, Jack, Lawrence, and Micheline is a certain factor of unbalance which involves the obligation to take oneself seriously and play the role needed to disguise the reality which would destroy.

This isolation is as much a cause as it is an effect. It is because all our cases were not loved during their early childhood that they were unable to love, as adults, in an oblative way, and to give and accept love. Sometimes it was that their parents were too strict, but most often it was because they were too possessive and indulgent and hence spoiled the children. These children were unable to feel "lovable" and therefore could not accept and give love.

One must love oneself a little in order to be able to turn toward others—to look at them and listen to them and learn to love them. If a person doesn't love himself, he spends his time looking at *himself*. How can he see others?

When one is compelled to play a role in order to conceal from oneself the conviction of one's own worthlessness, is it possible to love others? Scripture has expressed this, as it expresses everything, very well: "Love your neighbor as yourself." Note that one must love *oneself*.

The question might be raised, Aren't all these

unhappy people more or less at ease on their own in the role for which they have been compelled to rig themselves out? And we ask, in reply, what can an individual do on his own in this world where everything nowadays is achieved by teamwork, from the Olympic Games to the Nobel Prize; a world, moreover, into which the Lord has sent us to live with our brothers a life which is in the image of the life of the three divine Persons who are the One God?

We shall leave this question open, to be answered in another chapter.

[1] Joseph Folliet, *Invitation à la joie* (Paris,Centurion), pp. 9, 10, 11.

The Consequences of
a Lack of Self-confidence

PERSONAL CONSEQUENCES

*The lack of self-confidence involves an
incapability of accepting ourselves as we are*

For it is because we don't accept ourselves
that we lack confidence in ourselves—it is a
vicious circle!

It is because we did not have the unconditional and tender love of our parents, the only
ones who know how to love you "in spite of
everything"—and for the sole and sufficient
reason that you are their child—that the
foundations of our personality are off-center,
the structure of the affectivity balanced as pre-
cariously as a tightrope walker on his wire.

An individual must have been the recipient of
great tenderness in order to have traversed the
necessarily traumatizing stages of early childhood gainfully and to have acquired the solid
certitude that he was of value to someone—first

to his mother, then to his father, and finally, in brief, a value in himself.

This certitude makes it possible for us to accept ourselves with our shortcomings and defects, since it is clear that we have abilities and qualities as well.

Anne was enthusiastic, interested in everything; she had a quick and lively intelligence and a great need to share everything with others which made her very talkative. Throughout her childhood she was reproached for her chattering and even for her enthusiasm. She had to reach thirty before she discovered, with the help of a psychoanalyst, that this "defect" enabled her to teach in an exciting way and to give brilliant lectures.

This perception that a defect might at the same time be a quality enabled her to accept the idea that her volubility might be a nuisance to others by hindering them from expressing themselves. Once she had been given a sense of security, she was able to make the effort to keep quiet in order to listen, something she had never been able to accomplish before, when all she knew was that she was a "chatterbox."

Vincent, aged ten, was very uncommunicative. He did not seem happy among his brothers and sisters, who were much more relaxed and outgoing. He was the lowest achiever in the schoolroom, where he was held back by a constitutional slowness which left him far behind the others.

Then by a happy accident, his brothers being

away, his father gave him an odd job to tinker with and for the first time observed his manual dexterity, which was really extraordinary. From then on his father entrusted many small jobs around the house to him and always had him on hand as an assistant whenever he himself undertook something important.

In six months Vincent was completely transformed: he smiled, talked, and his schoolwork improved. The self-confidence he had acquired considerably diminished the slowness which had been holding him back.

There was Charlotte, who until she was around thirteen toiled miserably at school to produce compositions on which she received scarcely average grades. She was terribly inhibited about expressing herself; indeed, given the repressive attitude of her parents, she hardly ventured to have any ideas of her own. Then came the day when she produced an essay on a writer she really enjoyed. It was praised by her teacher, and it gave her insight into herself on this level. From then on she was among the best students in her literature courses. Eventually she took her degree in literature with distinction, and at thirty had become an important writer.

There was Charles, aged forty. For fifteen years he had been an engineer with the same firm, where he had advanced as far as he could go in view of an extreme timidity and lack of self-confidence. Unexpectedly, the sudden illness of his immediate superior forced him to move in as a substitute. He did so with great trepidation; indeed, poised for a leap into some other job. But under the pressure of necessity he revealed his real ability, much to the relief of his superior, who thereafter gave him full support. In ten years he advanced through all the administrative levels to which, in his false humility, he had long since ceased to aspire.

A very brilliant father had always overwhelmed Charles with his superiority, convincing him from his earliest childhood that he was no good at anything. He needed this providential occasion, and the intervention of his superior acting like a good father to him, to give him insight into himself, so that he could venture to accept his timidity as the other side of the quality which gave him his great professional skill.

In order to accept himself a person must know himself

A person can know himself in a static way, as Charles did: "I'm a timid person, so I'll never be able to forge ahead." Or he can know himself in a dynamic way: "This is the quality I have; this is the one I lack but must acquire."

Insofar as self-knowledge is a step toward some objective it is dynamic, positive and enriching, and it will make possible our acceptance of our negative traits.

"I talk much too much and haven't much capacity for listening to others. But I can establish contact with my students, my listeners. So I can also establish it by listening. Silence is becoming a need for me because I have discovered its value and its attractiveness.

"The very fact that I have found this out and accepted it is already an advance which, if I keep it in mind, will help me to accept myself more, and so to improve myself a little more easily."

Nevertheless it must be recognized that such dynamic self-knowledge calls for a little bud of confidence in oneself, and not everyone has made this beginning; but it can be made with the help of others if we will let them help us. Sometimes a little nudge is enough: "Oh, that's very good! That's beginning to look very much like a pyramid, darling!" And the small boy, delighted, manages to carry out his very hazardous project until the pyramid is complete.

The compliment which reassures us—how many of us can do without it? It helps even the best-balanced among us, for we all have our moments of self-doubt. As Marc Oraison puts it, dynamic equilibrium is like a bicycle; it stays upright only when it's on the move.

Father E. was an excellent preacher; his sermons had great substance as well as inspiration. The whole town was flocking to his parish, which he served with real love and, even more, with great humility.

One Monday morning I had occasion to ring him up in connection with preparations for our parents' meeting, and I took the opportunity to thank him for his sermon of the day before, from which I had profited in a special way. I found that he was astonished and anxious to know whether this was really true. I then described to him how the whole congregation had hung on his words, feeling that he had had a sudden inspiration from the Holy Spirit—we'd felt really bowled over. "You are doing me good," he said. "I had rather the feeling that I wasn't getting through."

Of course I lost no time in alerting other friends who, under one pretext or another, looked for the opportunity to say something to him about it. We were all amazed to learn that we could do him good and encourage him by telling him what we thought he was fully aware of.

Little boosts of this sort are even more necessary, and for a stronger reason, in the case of those whom an upbringing which was puritanical, or inflexible in some other way, denied compliments when they were due. For it is encouragement of this kind which gives a sense of security and a relaxed attitude toward life by contributing to the individual's sense of his worth.

There will be no need, then, to put on any front; we shall be able to be simply ourselves. This kind of assistance often makes it possible to approach that dynamic self-knowledge we have been discussing, of which we shall have more to say later on. However discouraged we may be, this achievement is possible for all of us if we are helped toward it. But once again: we can do nothing by ourselves.

The necessity of playing a role

However, if I do not have that necessary minimum of confidence in myself, if I doubt my own worth to the point of seeing only my inabilities, my defects, my faults, I will lose all hope of ever improving my situation. If I am the passive type, the danger is that I will "run true to form," corresponding to the image of myself which others reflect to me; or, taking the opposite course, I may unconsciously build up a role for myself to impose it on the credence of others, so that they will reflect to me the image of myself as someone of greater substance.

I may do both things at the same time.

This is the attitude which one always finds in maladjusted children. A child, for example, who has heard it said again and again that he is a lazy good-for-nothing has no recourse but to become one.

Or, on the other hand, an individual takes the course of "self-assurance" and unconsciously constructs the appearance of a more positive personality and tries as hard as he can to impose it on others, and above all to believe it himself.

Marian had been very much frustrated by her parents. They meant well by her, but they did not know how to love her. It was nothing they could help; they did what they could. As a result, she was completely lacking in self-confidence. She saw herself as rather unfeminine, clumsy with household tasks, abrupt in her gestures, too talkative. She had been told all these things since early childhood.

It took a very shrewd observer to see through her, for she made what might be called a production of her self-assurance: a loud voice, rapid and interesting speech, high spirits and a brilliant intelligence (which she had had to develop to compensate for the atrophy of her sensitivity).

When love revealed her to herself, her friends observed that her gestures became less abrupt, the tone of her voice gentler. She learned to listen instead of brandishing her own ideas like torches.

But this role deceives only those who are not very alert or highly perceptive, for the real inner attitude of such an individual is betrayed by a whole collection of very slight signs. And a sensitive person tries to understand because he pities these people, who are sometimes cordially disliked by everyone in their vicinity. The trouble is that they take themselves more seriously than anyone else does, and they can become really dangerous.

Catherine was a small blonde with a peach-bloom complexion, violet-blue eyes and a fragile appearance despite a rather full face whose features were well-defined. This fragile appearance was something she had deliberately cultivated in order to disguise her fundamental toughness. Under the flower-like exterior there was a will of iron.

Very much mistress of herself, she succeeded to some extent in concealing her authoritarianism. But if she was able to camouflage a certain crispness in her look by speaking softly, one sign of which she was unconscious betrayed her: her self-assurance and pride manifested itself in a habit of tapping her heels.

Everything about her was artificial and calculated, from the carriage of her head—chin well up so that she would not lose an inch of the height she thought inadequate—the well-modulated voice, deliberately charming and velvety, although its natural timbre (which made itself heard more often than she thought) was sharp and metallic.

She had three children, but she would have liked to have a larger family because she considered herself a "born educator." Highly dynamic—in fact, she was a real zealot—she compensated by finding an outlet in political and religious gatherings and succeeded in involving her husband as well. (His personality, which seemed mature enough, had been forced to abdicate, to the great disappointment of his relations and friends.) She turned herself into a trouble-shooter in the service of the elect, the clergy, whom she upbraided without hesitation for their lack of orthodoxy.

Regarding herself as the depository of sound faith, she made a study of theology with a view to ensuring its preservation in the diocesan catechisms. And she tried to infiltrate all the groups concerned with carrying out the Church's aggiornamento with the purpose of leading them back to a true concept of the faith—that is, to the contemplation of our last end and the fear of hell, which were the motive forces in her own religion.

She was not afraid to remonstrate with the bishops (and would have remonstrated with the pope, had the opportunity presented itself) about the latest papal encyclical, which was "too modernist" for her taste, having been "extorted from him by his Satan-inspired advisers."

Moreover, Satan was concerning himself with her with great perseverance: she discovered him in a strange noise which woke her in the night, in the unaccountable shattering of a little statue of the Blessed Virgin. She felt that in her humble way she was being the object of his attacks, like the Curé of Ars.

Imagining herself to be charged with a deep responsibility for the happiness and holiness of her whole family and all her friends, she wore them out by preaching the good news in season and out of season, urging them to make retreats and go to confession more often in order to avoid going to that hell which certainly awaited them except for the concern she showed for them.

Tiresome as she was for everyone, she was unbalancing for her children, whom she brought up in this fear of hell and at the same time with the notion that they were saints. Their education was no more open and balanced than her faith was adult and positive. It was impossible to discuss anything with her in either the political or the religious sphere; she had an answer for everything. A Madame de Stael and Joan of Arc rolled into one, she believed herself incapable of being mistaken.

Flawless in her own estimation—and, she assumed, in the sight of God and of Satan as well—she exuded an elaborately subtle kind of spitefulness when those around her failed to come up to her expectations. She tried, without success, to sow quarrels and hostility in her family, setting her brothers and sisters against each other, under the pretext—of course—of helping them to work out their salvation.

She was completely blinded by her own self-assurance, and she might have been almost diabolic if she had not been capable of an immense generosity. Her overconfidence resulted to a great extent from the combination of a passionate nature, a sense of deprivation in not having more children, and an emotional immaturity. All this had resulted, for the most part, from an upbringing that was strict, cautious, and lacking in vitality, a serious hormonal imbalance, and a drive to use her lively intelligence which was one aspect of her maladjustment.

She was as much pitied as feared, but people tended to steer clear of her.

It should be noted in passing that although there are many exceptions to this, women take themselves seriously less often than do men. The fact is that femininity is completely oriented toward maternity and motivated by it.

What, after all, is maternity—"mothering"—if

not that consciousness of little things, that en-
forced realism, which makes a woman notice the
slightest change in her nursling's cry, the hardly
perceptible difference in his color? It is an
awareness of little things which is an adherence
to what is real, and inevitably involves the perception of his littleness and his capabilities at
the same time, and also of the no more than
relative importance of everything which is not a
serious threat to his health—indeed everything
short of death, for which alone there is no
remedy.

When a woman takes herself seriously, it is
often because she has had to make up for some,
perhaps partial, damage to her affectivity by
overdeveloping her intelligence; and this development, deprived of the counterbalancing
development of her sensitivity, has made her
exclusively intellectual. The bluestockings have
been of this type—Madame de Stael, and others
such as Elizabeth the First of England, Catherine
of Russia, Christine of Sweden. They left their
names in history or letters, but they were formidable women who had destructive effects on
those around them and on themselves as well.

A man, on the other hand, is less realistic by
nature and more intellectual. His tendency
toward synthesis leads him to juggle with ideas,
even when he is confronted by the everyday
reality of facts. It is curious to observe how
characteristically masculine it is to come up with
an idea, first of all, and then to try to adapt

reality forcibly to this pattern which comes wholly out of his own head—and is not always inspired. Without the restraint of reality—which he has learned, in this way, to ignore—he is more tempted to believe that things have "actually happened." It is for him to "rethink the world," all the more when his emotional life has not been a success. Thus he finds compensation in order to be able to accept the failure which touches him most intimately.

Frank, Eric, Lawrence, and Jack would have been different if they could have permitted themselves to receive the love their wives offered them, which perhaps would have brought them the counterweight of their "success" and thus of their "realism."

The inability to accept either criticism or help

We play a role because we are forced into it by our unconscious, which, moved by a solid instinct of self-defense and self-preservation, tries to protect us from the poor opinion of ourselves that we cannot allow ourselves to have. The slightest criticism, since it threatens to unveil part of the truth to us—to strip off the bandage with which we unconsciously cover our wounded affectivity—quite demolishes us by calling into question some aspect of ourselves, or our whole selves.

This is the source of the extreme vulnerability of people who are full of self-assurance. They are like tightrope walkers who can be blown over by a strong gust of wind. It is also the source of the extreme aggressiveness which criticism arouses, an aggressiveness which is a reflex of self-preservation. It is vital insofar as its purpose is to preserve the precarious equilibrium which—through force of habit, through suffering, through cunning—our unconscious has often, after a fashion, succeeded in building up. Frequently this was a means of enabling us to survive the destruction or the mutilation of our affectivity, ill-treated by harsh childhood experience and by parents who were more often unaware of their effect than lacking in concern for us. We all know people, apparently sure of themselves, whom a word can deflate like a pricked balloon; or who, behind the facade of an aggressive intellectualism, reveal themselves as totally incompetent on the human level.

David has an aggressive beard, a dominating look, and the pretentious language of a schoolteacher who had somehow, by great effort, succeeded in getting a degree in psychology, which he had neither assimilated nor integrated.

Capable enough so far as testing a child and making a more or less valid diagnosis was concerned, he only blundered in treating those entrusted to his care, and he failed completely in the rearing of his own children, whom he begot for his exhausted wife at the rate of one a year.

On an occasion when he attended a lecture on psychoanalysis given to a very unsophisticated audience by a social worker, he found it

intolerable that she rejected all the words beginning "psy" which were so formidable to her
listeners and set forth the ABC's of in-depth
psychology in terms they could all understand.
He took it as a personal attack and went onto
the defensive.

Several months earlier, as a matter of fact, he
himself had given a lecture to social workers on
the same subject. An informed audience, they
nevertheless were quite unable to grasp what he
was saying, so much did he juggle ideas and revel
in high-flown phrases and find refuge behind
expressions involving the "libido," the "super-
ego" and "the Id," whose esoteric connotations
were his security. This esotericism enabled him
to make himself believe that he had assimilated
and understood the matter cf which he spoke; in
fact he had only a strictly intellectual knowledge
of it—and therefore, in a limited sense, he was
formidably informed.

Every attack on his vocabulary, which was
part of the character he had created for himself
(for this vocabulary surrounded his incompetence with a protective aura of conceit),
wounded him to the quick, since it called his
whole being into question. Hence his aggressiveness.

What a contrast was presented by a group of
educators interviewed on television who, though
they certainly had no degrees in psychology,
have for twenty years been devoting themselves
to maladjusted young people in conflict with
their environment. Asked: "Do you think you

are accomplishing something for these young people?" they replied, haltingly and with considerable hesitation: "Perhaps . . . we can't tell . . . we hope . . . . These young unwed mothers are teaching us a lot by the courage they demonstrate in raising their child. It's they who give us lessons in courage, not the other way round."

There was a certain psychoanalyst, very alert and observant, with a condescending smile and handshake, whose ready-made ideas about femininity—"A woman should like cooking and sewing"—were purely intellectual and not at all integrated. He let rare words drop oracularly, but he was quite unable to make his own wife happy; he had to leave her, and he showed himself equally incompetent in establishing another home.

Unable to put into practice for himself what he pretended to be helping others to discover, he unquestionably took himself more seriously than if he had been Freud. He was thoroughly unpleasant in all his encounters with others, overwhelming them with his self-sufficiency, and he could not tolerate the least advice from a better-qualified colleague.

By way of contrast there was another psychoanalyst, René Laforgue, with a world-wide reputation. His warm smile and his look, so full of goodness, were equalled only by the humility of a great man of science. In ten years of working with him I never saw him take himself seriously. Neither did he take himself for an oracle: he never stated anything in a way which brooked no argument. Everything he proposed took the form of a suggestion; it left room for error, for liberty and also for grace. This is the impression he made on all those who approached him during his lifetime and who continue to be sustained by his spirit and his example. Here is a model with whom one can identify. He gave everyone so much love!

What is psychoanalysis if not a work of love which resuscitates dead sensitivities, recalls hurt emotions to health, gives life to those who have been cut off from their better selves?

It is not by taking ourselves seriously that we do lasting work. We all know doctors who pose as "big bosses" because unconsciously they are afraid of their patient, or their own relative incompetence, and do not assume their responsibilities before there is danger of death. They too shelter behind a rampart of words which are cheering to themselves and tormenting for the unfortunate patients for whom "cephalic index," "epistaxis," and so on, are unknown qualities—gravely threatening if not incurable!

We have all been under those authoritarian professors who need to exact a ferocious discipline in order to make themselves obeyed, terrorizing their students because they are fundamentally lacking in natural authority and ill-at-ease in their own skins, so to speak, because they cannot accept themselves. Generally, this is because they are unconsciously aware that they are not up to their job, not having quite learned to handle it. The students catch onto it at once—hence the rows and hence the discipline.

By way of contrast:

Luke, a former officer with a degree in oriental languages, changed his career to teaching at the age of fifty. He spent all his leisure time "boning up" on the classics which the class was reading, so that he would be sure to be up to his job—whereas his immense culture would have allowed him to dominate the situation from a superior position. He never had to exercise disciplinary measures, except in the usual sense of keeping order in the class. The students were aware at once of the humility with which he faced his new job.

He did not take himself seriously, and he was accepted and obeyed from the start. The young have a clearmindedness which is distressing.

People like René Laforgue, like Luke, comfort us and give us a sense of security because they do not overwhelm us with their knowledge but know, on the contrary, how to listen to us, recognize us as persons—our lives, our interests, our worth.

People who take themselves seriously put themselves in the position of being quite unable to accept the criticism which would help them. They are not geared to accepting any contradiction whatsoever, since it calls them into question again, and this could be traumatic for the fragile

equilibrium they have built up from their disequilibrium. How, then, can they be helped to
improve themselves and divest themselves of the
role they are playing? We shall leave the question open, for discussion later on.

The inability to accept our failures

If criticism, often quite without malice, is
enough to disturb our uneasy balance and fill us
with self-doubt, what can be said of the tragic
effects of a failure?

For a balanced person, in harmony with himself, a failure is even more instructive than a
success, and a greater source of progress. He is in
a position to weigh it with a certain amount of
objectivity, to readjust his aim, giving it a greater
precision by bringing it into line with the realities this failure has revealed to him, and indeed
with reality in general.

The individual who takes himself seriously is
often badly shaken by a failure, because the
false equilibrium which he has constructed out
of his disequilibrium as a defensive measure cannot sustain such a test. How could it, since the
failure confronts him with the reality which he
repels, disguises, rejects or denies with all his
might, however unconsciously?

Stephen had been very much frustrated by a
father who always treated him in a way destructive for his morale. The reason was that the boy
was totally unlike his father, having instead his
mother's sensitive nature. As a consequence

Stephen was incapable of being a good father to his own children.

Fortunately he had a wife who was a born educator. She helped him to become aware of the serious mistakes he was making with regard to his eldest son. His attitude was a point-by-point imitation of his own father's attitude toward him. Every time she made him face up to his mistakes, he reacted with a tragic stance: "I'm an incompetent. I should go away; you'd be better off without me."

Eventually, thanks to the certain, solid and very confident love of the one who knew him best, he achieved a more positive attitude; but he was never able to rebuild the confidence in himself which his father had so badly undermined.

Clarence, the eldest son, "inherited" his father's lack of self-confidence. He was extremely vulnerable, and he was so depressed by any setback in school that he let it take away his interest in working to regain his lost standing. Each term he came closer to total defeat, until in the seventh grade he was on the verge of having to repeat a semester. At this point an understanding and warmhearted principal, providentially for the boy, played the role of a good father by having confidence in him. Clarence began to want to work; he discovered that he had a talent for mathematics; and he graduated with distinction.

His brother Bob, on the other hand, who was by nature more relaxed, was not his father's target, and he suffered less from the latter's involuntary mistakes. A headstrong boy, he clashed with his mathematics teacher in the eighth grade, and his work was so unsatisfactory that the teacher was opposed to his being promoted. The boy came close to despair.

His mother was able to help him to draw a lesson out of this failure which was so full of the possibility of unfortunate future consequences. He learned to master his impetuosity and stubbornness.

Since he was both intelligent and willing, he was able to establish a steadier control of himself and to give his teacher a practical demonstration of his ability, thus restoring the latter's confidence in him. After his final examinations, he was permitted to take a makeup examination in mathematics.

When we are geared to dealing with it in a balanced way, a setback can be very constructive.

Daniel was happily married to Marie, a delightful woman—pretty, sensible, well-bred and thoughtful. Since he was so sure of her, he left her every weekend to go hunting; worked late at night; neglected all those demonstrations of tenderness and kind attentions which prove to a woman that she is loved, and which she needs if she is to bloom as a woman and be happy.

Six years went by. Three children were born, even though he, egoist that he was, hadn't wanted any. Once they were there, owing to their mother's desire for them and her courage, he loved them tenderly and, according to his lights, well.

Then the inevitable happened. Marie met the "man of her life." He lavished attentions on her, gave her the shelter of his manhood, overwhelmed her with his tenderness and his sensitive concern for her—in other words, really loved her.

After several months of resistance she gave in to him and went off with him for eight days. On her return, she decided to get a divorce in order to marry him.

After a period of violent upheaval, Daniel discovered the degree to which he was attached to his wife. He agreed to a period of trial separation during which she would live alone with the children. And when this courageous woman realized that her duty, so far as her children's happiness was concerned, was to resume her conjugal life, she discovered with astonishment that Daniel could be a chivalrous husband, considerate and tender. He telephoned her several times a day, brought her flowers, paid her innumerable little attentions of which she had not thought him capable.

Daniel was revealed to himself through suffering, and he knew how to be instructed by his failure, thanks to his family and friends, who made him see his own grave responsibility for his wife's adultery. "You only got what you deserve. You asked for it, and it happened." This trial awakened his love and brought out qualities which had been dormant, buried under a layer of egoism that had prevented him from trying to understand his wife.

Divorce is a traumatizing failure, although in

a different way for a man than for a woman. A man usually reacts on the level of his vanity. That his wife would reject him to take back her freedom touches him at the most sensitive point of his pride. Blinded by chagrin, he often loses all his sense of paternal duty. He will persist in claiming his children in order to take them away from the mother as a mode of revenge. It is very difficult, not to say impossible, to make him realize his own faults during these months of crisis, so deep is the hurt. As a matter of fact, there are always faults on both sides.

The woman reacts on the level of her affectivity. The failure of her home strikes at the innermost center of her femininity. The fact that her husband is leaving her for another woman can make her lose all the confidence in herself that a happy union had consolidated.

Christine, aged forty-five, had been abandoned by her husband, a successful butcher. He wanted to marry his cashier, with whom he had been unfaithful to his wife for months. Christine had tried to avoid seeing it, out of a fear of reality and as a defense against something which would undermine the foundations of her personality.

However, the meanness of her husband's behavior eventually led her to ask for a divorce in order to preserve her three children's rights and her own. Her lawyer, as is customary in such cases, cautioned her: "Be very careful until the trial is over; do not take a lover. Your husband could catch you in the very act of adultery—he's only hoping for that—and you would lose all your rights."

The social worker in the case, who made a rapid appraisal of this still-young woman—serious, overwhelmed and indeed nearly annihilated by this failure—did not understand her well enough to insist on her being careful and to support her in it.

Six months later, at the very time when the social inquiry was being concluded in her favor, awarding her substantial alimony and the custody of her children, her husband had her caught in the act of adultery, much to the consternation of the social worker and her lawyer.

But on investigation they found her completely transformed and rejuvenated, in a state of full recovery. "Perhaps I have lost my divorce action," she said to them, "but I know that I can still interest a man enough for him to want to make me his mistress."

This adventure, although it had no future, was necessary for her in order to recover her self-confidence, her femininity, and her dynamism. Although she was deprived of a large part of the alimony of which she would have been able to avail herself a month later, she managed to set up a butcher shop in competition with her husband's, and she did very well in business before marrying again a year or two later.

She had needed that transitional lover in order to recover her self-confidence and her femininity.

It is possible that we may be capable of drawing lessons from a failure at the time it occurs, and yet be crushed by it later on, if our self-confidence has, for one reason or another, been shaken.

Jerome had been appointed by the head of his firm to the management of a branch of the business with which he was totally unfamiliar. On his arrival he was met by a crossfire of hostilities. His superior was furious at having such a young staff member sent to him from another city, when he usually recruited them himself. He was envious of the young man's academic degrees, which he himself lacked. A small-scale executive, not up to his responsibilities and made aggressive by the fact rather than otherwise—so he summed Jerome up.

On the other side was the hostility of his subordinates, in a fixed routine which they did not want to change. They all closed ranks against their new boss and refused to improve their work, partly through a lack of conscience and of professional standards, but also through a fear of responsibilities.

After a year's work in this atmosphere Jerome's balance sheet was weighed on the side of liabilities. His superior was as hostile toward him as ever, and since he refused to receive him for conferences, Jerome was in the position of having to convince him wholly by actions. But actions were made difficult by the policy of spiteful inertia which had been adopted by his colleagues, and they had the boss's ear.

The initiatives he undertook in making contacts were also unsuccessful. The clients of this branch office were socially inflexible and lacking in cordiality; they refused all dialogue with "this inexperienced youngster" whom they didn't know. They were hardly more distrustful of the commercial travelers they saw once a week—and it took years before these salesmen could gain the confidence of the community.

In the meantime Jerome had made a very happy marriage, which had brightened his whole outlook on life. When, at the end of the year, he wrote his annual report, he did it in a very objective way, drawing lessons from his failures on every level for the benefit of his superior and of the president of the firm. With regard to his superior: he admitted that he should have tested the terrain before having himself appointed to the staff. With regard to the clients: he acknowledged his error in wishing to enter into dialogue with such a distrustful milieu before making the kind of psychological and sociological study which would have acquainted him with its problems, so that he would know how to listen. With regard to his colleagues: he criticized his own lack of patience, his clumsy attempts at dialogue which took their aggressiveness insufficiently into account (an aggressiveness motivated by his background, his youth, his being an import, and so on).

It was a very positive reaction to his failure, and it made it possible for Jerome to enter into dialogue with his superior if not with his colleagues.

Three months later a serious crisis in his marriage called everything into question again by destroying at its basis the self-confidence which his love had given him. This failure in the emotional sphere, against which he reacted by hardening himself, made his position inflexible, so that he lost all the good will he had derived three months earlier from his objectivity toward himself.

The fierce hostility of his subordinates was reawakened by his weakness, which they sensed, and they joined forces with his superior, whose aggressiveness got the upper hand again. It was indicated to Jerome that he was "undesirable at the branch office." This, on top of his emotional failure, caused him to go into a serious depression from which he emerged only eight months later.

The sterility of a couple can also be a failure, and it is especially difficult for the husband to accept it if he is the one responsible.

Paul and Jacqueline had become desperate at having no children after five years of marriage. The gynecologists found that Jacqueline was perfectly normal, but when Paul was examined it was discovered that he was the reason for the sterility of their home.

Paul was both distressed and resentful. He lost all his high spirits and his zest for life; he became aggressive toward his wife, making her exceedingly unhappy. He also did badly in his job. Then one day a doctor advised him to adopt a child and sent them to an adoption service to be interviewed.

Seven hours of in-depth conferences with the couple brought the husband to the point of expressing his feeling of impotence (in the radical sense of the word) and therefore of worthlessness: "What use am I, anyway, if I can't even have children to continue my line?"

At first he was opposed to the intrusion of any "strange" child in his home, but after several weeks and several interviews with the social worker he admitted that fundamentally, if an adopted child would make his wife happy, he was willing. Then he came progressively to accept the idea that this child would also be his and that it would be no great strain for him to reveal to it its origins. He realized that he would be able to rear it with a concern for the vocation it would develop, and not according to the pattern of "the child that would surely have been his."

Only the integrated acceptance of their sterility on the part of adoptive parents makes it possible for them to tell the child the truth about its origins without traumatizing it, because then they have genuinely accepted it as not being born of them.

This trial, endured by the two of them together, united the couple at a deeper level, enlivened their faith, and made them into the cheerful and well-balanced foster parents of three lovely children who were entrusted to them and whom they brought up in an atmosphere of tenderness and respect for their liberty which enabled them to develop and grow harmoniously.

SOCIAL CONSEQUENCES

People who are forced to take themselves seriously readily become intolerable to those around them, as we have seen in the cases of Frank, the priest, Miss Durand, and Catherine. Often tyrannical and authoritarian, very ready to take offense, they do not accept any criticism and, as we have noted, it is impossible for them to work as part of a team and to live in harmony with their family or professional environment.

Catherine wanted to lay down the law in her family under the pretext of helping every member to achieve his salvation. Antoinette decided the fate of her friends and pushed a nervous girl into a relapse.

If these poor individuals who take themselves so seriously don't have the chance to become heads of state or even presidents of their firms, their situation soon becomes uncomfortable, for they are more or less openly rejected by those around them. They are relegated to a solitary job; their families fear them and keep them at a distance; their children avoid them; they find themselves more isolated even than they subconsciously hoped for in wanting to put themselves on a pedestal.

From the moment when their unconscious chose isolation, they felt a failure—insofar as they did not blind themselves further, through anguish, into self-congratulation and self-glorification: "I'm misunderstood. It's normal—the others are so stupid." This impermeability to all criticism, and hence to all help, prevents them from profiting by what others have to offer them, and they become frozen, hardened in their position.

No improvement is open to them, for dialogue is no longer a possibility. And when one does not advance, one falls back. As in other matters, popular wisdom expressed this long ago.

Taking oneself seriously becomes a real danger insofar as this attitude increasingly cuts the victim off from other people and from reality, obliterating all objectivity and realism, so that he suffers a loss of effectiveness. When we take ourselves seriously we are often prevented from surrounding ourselves with able collaborators who will carry our enterprise on, as we saw in Frank's case.

Teamwork is the only realistic approach to our undertakings, whether in the affairs of the state, in a hospital, a business or, above all, a family. Working in a team—that is, within the framework of a group united by the common desire to go beyond the reflexes of self-esteem and egoism—is impossible for someone who does not accept himself as he is and whose self-esteem is consequently very much exposed to pinpricks. People who are full of self-assurance are able to accept neither criticism (because it casts all in doubt) nor any limits to their own competence;

and so teamwork is removed from the realm of possibility.

When a person knows everything better than anyone else, how can he avail himself of the help of someone working at his side, even if the latter's technique is quite different? We have to put up with these many-talented (in their own view) individuals whose judgment in any matter whatsoever is without appeal and whose opinions are definitive. They are feared as much as pitied, and we keep out of their way as much as we can. To be obliged to work with a superior or a colleague of this type calls for real sanctity!

As we have said before, if an individual cannot work in a team nowadays, what can be accomplished? Every job requires collaboration, the union of diverse talents, of complementary techniques, of diversified subject matter. One individual brings to the project his intuition and powers of analysis, another his capacity for synthesis and his realism. This one will contribute the reality of concrete facts from which that one will derive inferences with respect to knowledge and method. One will supply his reflectiveness and his moderation; the other his ease of expression and his enthusiasm; and a team working very effectively in harness is the result.

So it is at the operating table: the control of the patient's respiration is in the hands of the anesthetist; the patient's life is in the hands of the surgeon, depending on the precision and rapidity of their movements; in the hands, too, of the nurse, quick and precise in passing to him the right instrument, or the clamp needed to stop bleeding. Meanwhile the monitor, its dial turned, follows the course of the lancet. And some obscure aide has sterilized all the instruments and verified the fact that they are in prime condition.

In America, much more than in Europe, this equality of the members within the framework of the team has been long understood, so that the nurse's importance is usually seen as on a par with that of the doctor.

One of my friends, director-general of UNICEF programs in New York, was rather startled by this in the beginning, particularly by the casual attitude of the young secretaries toward her (she was in her sixties and a Canadian). "I'm sure they call me by my first name when they're talking about me," she said. "I'll have to get used to it. But how would I manage the project of working out these programs on a global scale if my pool of secretaries and stenographers were not equal to the task and did not feel involved in my work? Without them I can't do anything."

Hers is the right attitude, much more so than that of the doctor who makes a habit of preceding his nurse through every door because he is "the chief"—forgetting, because he is in the hospital, the courtesy he shows outside it.

The same goes for the parish priests with their assistants, the heads of businesses with their staff, and foremen with their workmen. One asks why the morale of a given enterprise is deplorable, why ill humor and ill will manifest themselves on every level: on closer inspection one often notices that everyone there takes himself seriously, from the janitor who wants to be a superintendent all the way to the president who wants to exercise the divine right of kings, and all the way down through the department heads and the employees at every level.

Each one of them provokes aggressiveness and puts those around him on the defensive: it is a chain reaction from the top to the bottom.

This situation is difficult to reverse. It requires all the art in nondirective therapy of a Carl Rogers if a staff team is to come into being which will accept, and work out and put into practice, the opposite principles, to the end result that each member will feel "good" in his own place and not want a position beyond his capabilities, and that all will work in a happy and relaxed atmosphere (which is not, one suspects, without relation to the productivity of the enterprise).

Is it possible for parents who take themselves seriously to have a well-balanced family? In the beginning there is a drama acted out between the marriage partners. We all know those omnipotent husbands who propose to teach everything to their docile wives, from the art of diapering the baby to the techniques of timing the roast and making the money "that they give them" go as far as possible.

Is this a couple, in the true sense of the word, or a team, or a marriage? It isn't even an association, for one has more respect for an associate. Sometimes a guardianship, where only one is supposed to be an adult and the other is definitely a minor, comes into being in the husband's role because the wife finds a certain comfort in it—in the surrender of all her responsibilities.

We know the inevitable consequences for the children of such couples, neither of whom is very adult emotionally.

How are the poor youngsters to find the means of developing themselves, without emotional conflict, in such a home? There is scarcely any recourse for them except to become like lost lambs, with no consistent personality development (as parents they themselves will be disastrous). Or else they can settle down into a position of permanent and systematic opposition which will preserve them as personalities but will be of little use so far as the attainment of emotional maturity is concerned. One does not build oneself up "against" reality but "with" and "for" it; when development takes place in opposition to reality and in spite of it, inflexibilities and rigidities inevitably result from which marriage partners and offspring—not to mention coworkers—will suffer later on.

One can develop oneself harmoniously in a positive, progressive way only in a milieu which is supportive, and hence affectionate; when love is adult—for this alone constitutes the security of which the child has the utmost need.

If it is possible to forge personalities in circumstances which are quite the opposite (and François Mauriac in his *Face to Face*, speaking of the Jansenist education he had received, applies this to Catholic writers) considerable damage is also involved: immature individuals blocked in their development, maimed in their sensitivity and intellectually aggressive—in short, all the forms of defense which an assaulted sensitivity has at its disposal.

Of course it is possible for grace to produce saints on the foundation of sensitivities which were disturbed in early childhood, as witness St. Ignatius Loyola and St. Therese of the Child Jesus; but it is the clearly understood responsibility of parents to facilitate God's work by supplying their children with a normal, adult affectivity, which helps them toward attaining the maturity of their faith.

Taking oneself seriously, as we have seen, considerably restricts our lives in society, in our work, in our families: these are the grave social consequences of this grave illness. We must become aware of it to help ourselves, if we are in danger of falling into this error, and to help others, with all our love, and with skill and humor as well, to realize and to remedy it, since everyone around them suffers from a similar malady.

Mental Hygiene

THE EDUCATION OF CHILDREN

The role of others

As we know, education must be based on building up the emotional maturity of the small child, an emotional maturity which will permit him to attain that dynamic self-knowledge that involves self-confidence.

This maturity, as we have seen, is built, so to speak, stone by stone from the time of the infant's birth, through a comprehension of his emotional needs—the distress he experiences at the changes represented by weaning, toilet training, the painful transition of the oedipal phase, school days, puberty, and finally adolescence.

We have repeatedly observed the extent to which a tender love must be matched, very early, by the authority which is its natural complement. We love "well" only if we are equally faithful in correcting. So popular wisdom discovered long ago, as it has discovered everything else.

However, we shall stress the role which "others" play in the harmonious traversing of all these stages, which are so many steps toward the plane of emotional maturity. This plane is, for the Christian, only a preparation for the definitive birth into eternal life—the destiny for which he believes that he has been created and redeemed.

A person does nothing by himself.

Although during the first months it is the mother who plays the essential role, very soon both parents enter in.

The father becomes very important quite early, with his role (an indirect one, if you wish to put it that way) of encouraging the mother and making her happy, enabling her to be receptive to the child's needs and available for all the tenderness the infant expects of her. This role becomes more direct when the child becomes aware of the father as the one who provides protection and security for the home, the figure in whose shadow nothing evil can befall him.

At the time of weaning, distressing for the child, who is alarmed by this new event in a domain so rich in emotional values, and frustrating for the mother—especially if she is breast-feeding—it is the father who brings comfort and reassurance to the mother faced with the refusals or whims of the unwilling infant; for the first time he manifests his personality in terms of opposition.

It is the same at the time of toilet training. The father joins the mother in congratulating the child and shows how proud he is when the mother tells how clever the child has been in this particular achievement which is so important for his future.

At the time of the thorny transition of the oedipal phase, the father assumes a role of primary importance to the working out of his son's virility and his daughter's femininity. On the other hand, it is the love of the parents as a couple, experienced by the child, which enables him, as we have seen, to find his place in the family triangle and to become aware of himself as a personality distinct from the parental couple, with a subconscious but already very strong aspiration toward the being who, later on, will form a couple with him.

The birth of brothers and sisters teaches the child that his mother's love can be shared without its being thereby diminished. The friction arising from contact with characters, personalities, and groups and subgroups which form and then separate in this little world of the family rubs the child's personality smooth, as it were, prepares him for life, and builds up his self-confidence.

The preparation for life is begun quite definitely when he enters school, where he discovers—often in a brutal and distressing way—the rule of life in society, its cruelty, its depersonalization, and its treasures of comradeship and friendship as well.

Friendship will help the adolescent to pass over that long, tragic stage which takes him from the equilibrium acquired during his earliest years and lost at puberty to the new equilibrium of adulthood (as the butterfly laboriously and painfully breaks away from its chrysalis).

There is friendship with his peers, with whom he merges and tries to blend in order to find a little of the security he has so totally lost; friendship with those a little older than himself—various instructors, scout leaders, club directors, who often serve as a bridge between him and his parents.

Fellowship and friendship will soon prove themselves insufficient for his youthful emotions, which are enthralled with the absolute, with exclusivity. In a few years they will be in search of Love, though dreading it all the while. This is the age at which young girls of thirteen or fourteen fall in love with their teacher or with an entertainment idol, one as inaccessible as the other—which they find very reassuring. Or boys dream, without daring to mention it to even their best buddy, of a friend of their sister's or of their mother's, who is also inaccessible for the same reassuring reasons.

When the age of marriage arrives—so soon

there is hardly time to notice it—the young man will be intoxicated by the discovery of that other whom he believes to have been born for him, and who enables him (insofar as being loved reveals him to himself) to be finally, completely himself through the love she bears him.

"While I am alone," says Pensée in Claudel's *Le Perè humilié*, "I am someone with no body at all, no position, no face. Only when someone comes . . . ."

The state in which emotional maturity has been reached, or fully attained, can be defined in this way: the young person has become capable of loving the other for his or her self and of receiving from the other a love that is free.

For that, one must oneself be sufficiently free, weaned emotionally, having completed one's growth—that is, emotionally independent of one's parents—and hence sufficiently independent to be loved.

Marc Oraison explains it well:

A person is never too close to someone he loves . . . nevertheless he must be careful not to "invade" or "encumber" him.

In this very nearness of hearts one must be able to keep his distance from the other, so that he will be able to see his place in the relation.

One must be able to establish that "cleavage" which alone makes the presence of one to the other a possibility.

Moreover, it is insofar as one does not feel threatened by any impossible unconscious demand on the part of the other that one can sustain the relation.[1]

Love of neighbor—all the more if he is the person who loves us—does not consist in annihilating oneself or in "dissociating oneself from oneself." It is not a question of "forgetting oneself" for the other, which actually means nothing; it is a question of thinking oneself and willing *oneself* in function of the other, for him and for oneself, distinctly.[2]

But this relation has its ups and downs even for the most well-suited couple:

We all have our "bad days" with regard to total emotional security in our confrontation with the other .... Our difficulties in being with the other should not surprise us; they are normal, though they may seem to us to be bizarre and embarrassing.[3]

Running parallel to the partnership of marriage, the professional world will help the young man to take his place in society and assume his civic responsibilities; it will serve, moreover, as an index of emotional maturity and give him confidence in himself. For each of the partners this self-confidence is perfected by their crowning achievement—the birth of the first child and of other children. This is so for the wife because she achieves it in the fullness of her femininity, which, as we have seen, maternity signifies; for the husband because it assures the continuance of his name—which is infinitely reassuring and cheering to him.

In the course of all these stages it is other persons who have contributed to the building up of the adult; from his parents to his own child, they have supplied him with that confidence in himself which prevents him from taking himself seriously, because he knows and accepts himself in his relativity. The other—more precisely, others—are thus essential factors in the harmonious construction of the individual. And it is because an individual lacked the fortunate circumstance of being helped by others that he is impelled to take himself seriously, and hence to isolate himself from these others, whom he fears.

Don't we always fear what we don't know?

Respect for the child's innate sense of humor

Humor is innate in the child, inasmuch as it consists in the expression of his clear-eyed outlook on things and beings and his astonishment at our inconsequentialities and inconsistencies.

Here is a universally familiar kind of childish questioning which is quite typical:

"Daddy, why are black plums red?"

"Because they're green."

Francis, two and a half, looked me up and down with his big grave eyes when his mother introduced me to him, and then said, "Why isn't there a mister?"

Since grownups are the frequent targets of children's remarks of this sort, they often produce a state of insecurity—an insecurity directly proportionate to the clarity and the truth they express. Hence parents, who, it must be admitted, have a decided tendency to take themselves seriously in the presence of their children, cannot bear it, and before long they have maimed that innate sense in their children by rebuking them sharply when they manifest it. Such parents explain their attitude by saying that the child's candor is bad manners—if not sin! But their reaction is as mistaken as it is dangerous for the maturation of the small child's faith. And it is a crime to deprive our children of this faculty which is the salt of life, adds color to our everyday existence, and is an important factor in our equilibrium.

In fact it is humor—as we shall see later on when we discuss it more fully—which enables us to preserve our detachment with regard to others, to events, and to ourselves. It is the source of the perspective in which things appear as relative, of objectivity—in short, of realism. This realism makes us put things, persons, trials, where they belong in the context of the world, society, and our own lives.

Parents should be anxious to preserve this innate sense in their children. There is nothing to prevent their explaining that some remarks are not to be made in a loud voice, because they may hurt the feelings of the people they concern. But, for God's sake, let the children express themselves within the family circle, and let us be able to laugh at what they say. And let us accept their candor in all humility when we are their victims, thanking heaven for helping us, by means of these impertinent tots (our family's version of Dennis the Menace), not to take ourselves seriously. Thank heaven, too, for giving these children the faculty of reducing the phoniness of life.

What a priceless treasure that is! And how difficult it is to acquire it, once it has been lost.

THE EDUCATION OF ADULTS

The relativeness of emotional maturity

It is always possible for us to improve ourselves, to become aware of our emotional immaturity with respect to one point or another of our affectivity, to acquire confidence in ourselves by learning to know ourselves better. We are enabled to do this by other people. Knowledge of self by the self must pass through others also.[4]

Wasn't Louis XIV the greatest king France had ever known even though he suffered from a marked Oedipus complex?

Wasn't Napoleon a keen strategist and an administrative genius, although it seems that a failure complex led him to scuttle a great part of what he had constructed?

To take a case closer to the ordinary run of human beings:

Miss Bourges is a fifty-year-old nurse, full of vitality and high spirits. One day a social-worker friend confided to her that since she often worked until eight o'clock in the evening, she took an unauthorized weekend off, from time to time, beginning on Friday night. "You can do that?" was the nurse's startled reaction. "I never could! I'd be too afraid of retribution. I'd be sure that God would send me an accident!"

This woman, whose courage had withstood every test during the war and who took on the gravest responsibilities daily in her nursing career, had remained on the infantile level in her religion. For her, God was the judge; the cop who has you under surveillance—and then Wham! He sticks you with a ticket for jay-walking the moment you put your toe over the white line.

Miss Bourges lacked emotional maturity on this precise level, and—it would seem—in this sector exclusively.

There was Bernard, a contractor—virile, dynamic, a realist in business matters, seemingly endowed with perfect balance. Yet when he celebrated his fortieth birthday he was in the process of receiving his third divorce because he was incapable of making a woman happy.

Gerald: a man who begot a child of his wife every eleven months because he was unable to

master his instincts in this area, although every-
where else in his life he demonstrated re-
markable self-control.

There was Lucille, the mother of a family and
a businesswoman—organized, balanced, very
feminine and diplomatic. Nevertheless she
brooded over her four-year-old son, overwhelming him with so much solicitude that he
was in danger of becoming a psychological crip-
ple.

Bernard, Gerald and Lucille have a section
missing in their emotional maturity: the structure looks solid to the eyes of the uninitiated,
but for the more perceptive it shows a gaping
hole in the foundations which will some day be
the cause of a serious crack in the building.

This does not prevent them from functioning
in an apparently normal way, from taking on
risks and responsibilities (as we have seen in the
cases of Eric, Jack, Lawrence, and so on), from
being virile or feminine persons. But their emotional life is cracked, their sensitivity maimed or
atrophied or amputated, as the case may be, in a
more or less important sector. The day they
become aware that that is where the cause of
their marital or educational difficulties lies, a
great step forward will have been taken. This
knowledge will be dynamic if they use it to
improve themselves and to cross the stage—
perhaps the one they lack—to achieve the human
totality of their maturity.

*The help of others in this dynamic
self-knowledge*

We shall be assisted toward the attainment of
this awareness by life, by events, by trials, or by
other people.

Aided by dialogue and interaction with
people, others have managed to emerge from
their tangled psychological jungle. Alone, it is a
wasted effort; with others it is possible.[5]

For it is a truth that is proved every day: . . .
all interpretation or misinterpretation is trans-
formation. . . . As our environment interprets us,
so will it make us to be, owing to a terrible hold
which no brainwashing approaches.[6]

But this environment, if it regards us favor-
ably, also shows us the model which it gives us the
means of attaining.

The look of someone who loves me enhances
my freedom and assists at the birth of the real
man I am: it is creative.[7]

For lack of a kind person who knows how to
say, "You paint, write, speak well; you are so
likeable," how many people are unsure of themselves and never give all they have to give?[8]

How many of us still suffer from a Puritain
upbringing which forbade all compliments because they would make us vain?

Indeed we may be closer to ourselves than is
anyone else, and yet we cannot do without the
gold standard constituted by the *opinion of*

others to know definitely what our situation is.[9]

To know himself, a man needs to be known, to be recognized—in brief, to be accepted and loved as he is.[10]

This need which we have discovered in the infant persists in the adult, and does so all the more strongly if it has remained unsatisfied in early childhood.

In the words of Carl Rogers, the master of nondirective psychology:

When he finds someone who listens to him and accepts his feelings, the patient becomes capable, little by little, of listening to himself . . . lending an ear to the feelings which he had always repressed.

Gradually, as he learns to listen to himself, he comes to accept himself better. He finds himself able to escape from the facade behind which he had sheltered himself, to abandon his defensive behavior, to be more openly that which he really is. Gradually, as changes are made in him (becoming aware of himself by first accepting himself, and adopting a less defensive and more open attitude), he finally finds himself free to change and develop himself.[11]

Claudia was reproached for being too much of a dreamer, and hence too thoughtless and absentminded. She acknowledged this and also admitted that it jeopardized the team with which she worked in the management of a school for social workers.

This distressed her and prevented her from

being outgoing in her relations with this team.

A study of group dynamics enabled her to observe that whereas her absentmindedness embarrassed her to a certain extent it was also of considerable assistance to her personally inasmuch as it was a kind of openness. Indeed the distraction for which she was reproached enabled her to see a whole series of imponderables which put her, in depth, on the same interior wavelength as a great number of her students. When she could get hold of herself sufficiently to express herself at work meetings, she brought a crop of valuable insights to the team.

Becoming aware of this within the group with which she worked helped her to become more confident in accepting this absentmindedness and hence more able to express herself and to put at the service of the others all that this apparent absence of mind enabled her to register in depth—all the imponderables, all the dynamism, which the silence of listening contains.

Learning to accept oneself is acquired

Man, who is a free being, is always in a dynamic position in relation to himself if he wants to be and has the opportunity to be. However, anxious people, people in distress, adopt a rigid position in relation to themselves out of a need for security.

This acceptance of oneself, like self-knowledge, is acquired through others.

How about introspection? you say. Yes, that is most evidently a means, but it is very often a deceptive one, because I myself am the surest barrier between the self and myself. And if we have an unconscious need of playing a role in order to survive, the unconscious barriers often harden, and present the images of ourselves that we want to find. Moreover, introspection is more often depressing and discouraging than dynamic. Frequently, indeed, it reveals only what Sarano has called the "tangled junglc," where all the paths to the clearing have been lost in the undergrowth. We thrash about in vain; it is the kind of static self-knowledge that leads nowhere if not to the loss of confidence in ourselves.

Nevertheless there are positive as well as negative forces in all of us—virtues as well as defects. Given that Louis XIV and Napoleon—and Jack and Eric and the others—could have been what they were although they lacked emotional maturity in some respects, why shouldn't we be the same on our own scale?

Doesn't it help us to undertake this project without too much distress if we are aware that three-fourths of mankind, for various reasons, is lacking in this emotional maturity, which is constantly in need of being built up and improved, if not to be consolidated?

The balance we are aiming for will be made much easier to achieve if we have someone to help us by serving as a mirror and as a catalyst, perhaps by merely knowing how to listen.

If we keep in mind Baden-Powell's dictum about the five percent of good, which seemed to him sufficient foundation for rebuilding the other ninety-five percent, we can be encouraged to do it.

At forty Louise discovered that she was not in the right job; the teaching profession was giving her no outlet for her talents. Her painful maladjustment made her difficult to live with for those around her. With the assistance of a friend she became aware of her state. She took courageous action, going on half pay in order to attend an institute of cinema arts, where within three years she was trained for a career in the direction and production of films.

She had a rough time of it during those three years when her income was at the subsistence level, but she managed to bring it off, and now she is very happy in her work. Her whole personality has changed; she is serene and patient.

What she had learned to do was to draw up a balance sheet listing her needs, her possibilities, and the things for which she had a deep liking, and on the basis of this to change her whole orientation. And she did it in the face of virulent opposition from her whole family, for whom her leaving the Mother represented by the school system was childishness and folly.

Lucille, on whose problems with her son (over whom she brooded like a mother hen) we have already touched, became aware that her attitude might have serious consequences for the child. She consulted a psychotherapist and came to the realization that her attitude was motivated by her own relation with her father. He had always been brutal and hard toward her mother and herself, and it was this brutality which she wanted to spare her son—at the risk of making him effeminate.

She responded well to a little psychological treatment, and it enabled her to modify her attitude.

In the six months which followed, her son made much progress in the development of his masculinity. This was possible for him only because his mother had been willing to see the mistakes she was making in his upbringing and was able to remedy them.

Marcia, learning to drive, was having all the trouble in the world in the effort to shift gears. She seemed to be afraid of them, with the result that she often produced a screeching noise; this only increased her trepidation, and she reacted by bringing more force to the operation.

A reassuring remark from her driving instructor finally made her relax: "You know, grinding the gears never broke anything. It just can't be done!" Suddenly she realized that she was reacting unconsciously to the howls her father used to let out when he was trying to teach her to drive when she was sixteen. He had been very impatient with her and terrified her by making her think that she was going to wreck his car if she ground the gears.

This same Marcia could not manage to swim without becoming breathless until one day, in the course of a conversation with her brother, she suddenly recognized the fact that this fear went back to their early childhood when their father tried to teach them to swim by force. Although he had promised to hold her up, he had let her go, and she had swallowed a mouthful of water—to the vast amusement of that born educator. Thus at six years of age she had developed a terror of the water.

Once this fact was recognized and put back in its place, she could relax in the water, breathe normally and find real joy in swimming. Once again she had to accept the fact that—now forty—she was still under the tutelage of that father who had been so truly an educator, though not in the sense he intended.

On these very localized levels her emotional maturity had remained blocked, at five or at six years of age, the age at which the father—especially if he is brutal or impatient, and yells—can symbolize the ogre instead of security.

She would never have arrived at this realization alone: these attitudes of her father had traumatized her too much and had been too deeply buried in her unconscious. She had "repressed" them. It was in "expressing" them that she liberated herself from this unconscious and tyrannical tutelage and the distress it had entailed until she was forty.

The help of others is essential

The help of others will be manifested in the first place by the criticism earned by our behavior.

All criticism contains some positive element, even if it is made without objectivity, out of malice and with the desire to hurt. An oriental sage said that our enemies serve us better than our friends if we could but see the truth of that with which they reproach us.

Of course the most well-balanced person has his good and bad moments; and certain cruelties, when we are floundering, have the effect of pushing our heads underwater again. Is it possible for a drowning person to reflect on his plight and draw lessons from it?

"You only write to make money, don't you?" said a well-meaning friend to Sarah. He was escorting her to an appointment with a psychiatrist who was trying to draw her out of a severe depression she had been fighting for months. She was in doubt about everything, and of course doubted her own talent and the message she was capable of communicating.

"You only write to make money, because you're too intelligent to believe what you wrote to your girl friend the other day about what you have to bring to the world." (He laughed sarcastically.) "People can be such abominable flatterers!"

This cruelty, subtly worked out by a married couple bent on making Sarah face up to reality, and served up to her in a preaching tone, naturally ruined all the effects of the treatment, and the whole thing had to be started all over again. Sarah, full of self-doubt and guilt, quickly added this conviction to all those with which she was crucifying herself. She was only interested in money, and what she had written over a period of ten years had never helped anyone!

Under the circumstances, it was impossible for her to draw any lesson whatsoever from this criticism, which was nothing but spite—for the sake of her salvation, of course!

When that phrase, as cruel as it was ridiculous, came back into her memory months after her recovery, and struck home again despite the efficacious help (!) of the couple in question, she was able to turn it over in her mind and look at it from every angle in an attempt to find some positive value in it . . . and any excuse for it. Have you ever seen an author write serious books without wanting to touch the meager royalties they usually bring in?

This is an exterme case, involving an unkindness bordering on the fiendish in the circumstances, and motivated by a half-conscious desire to destroy what the couple envied in Sarah—while they pretended, to others, that they were doing everything (generously) to assist her recovery. Objectivity is what is required to make criticism beneficial, and it is what a depressed or ailing person is incapable of. Hence great precautions must be taken in criticizing the actions of such individuals—even with objectivity—for it must be understood that everything is an instrument of torture for them.

Apart from these extreme cases, people who take themselves seriously can learn first to accept criticism, then to desire it as an instrument of progress. They must learn to discern which criticisms are valid and to develop the objectivity with which criticism in general can and *ought to be* received.

This will be all the easier for us if the same criticism comes from several persons, from different sides. One person could have an animus towards us, but if several put the accent on the same point, isn't there some chance of their being right? We ought to make a slight examination of conscience in this light—to accept ourselves on that point.

Who is perfect?

Who is never mistaken?

Who is totally adult before the beginning of eternal life?

Well, then. . . .

But it is not easy to listen to others, to develop the capacity to "hear" what they want to—and can—tell us.

If we are to be listened to and *able* to listen, much love is called for.

As we have noted repeatedly, when someone is playing a role, it is usually because he cannot do otherwise, since he is forced into it by a powerful unconscious need. He is under the necessity of camouflaging reality for himself, of blinding himself—with regard to what? With regard to his sense of worthlessness, his conviction of his own incapacity for action, for effectiveness—or, worse, for loving.

The certainty that all these things were true would be such a death sentence for the sensitivity and the whole personality that the unconscious spares no effort in establishing the opposite: whence the role we are constrained to play in order to give to others the idea of ourselves which we *need* to have them reflect to us. This need is so imperious, so powerful, that it outmaneuvers everything that could prove the contrary to us.

Haven't we all known doctors suffering from cancer whose condition was evident even to neighbors knowing nothing about the subject, and yet they concealed their condition from themselves until the end? They are blinded by an instinct for self-defense which is as strong as life, and often it is a grace.

Don't we know those individuals who— despite every proof to the contrary—persist in believing in the love of the persons they themselves love?

"This last thing you did and said was just too much—it's all over between us. You are impossible!" So read the letter written to John by the girl he loved and who he believed loved him.

John, on his side, resisted his rejection. Overwhelmed by it one day, he would take courage the next, in order to prove to himself and to others that Marguerite had been put up to writing that way by her family, who rejected him because of their difference in social background. And he rebuilt the illusion that he was loved, because it was vital to him. He had always been frustrated in love, and he had the need to believe that finally he had been accepted and loved.

He had to meet Love—real and unconditional this time—before he was able to think clearly and to discover, with bewilderment, that when one loves, a gesture, a word, cannot be "too much"—much less, irreparable.

In the light of Agnes' love, and because she loved him in spite of his being "impossible," he understood that for three years he had nourished an illusion which had had profoundly destructive effects on him and had certainly taken its toll of his health; but at the same time it had helped him to survive some very trying experiences which he had had to endure from other sources.

This illusion had been the plaster cast which enabled him to carry on "operation survival" until the Lord should place on his path the individual who could save him—could enable him to leave his frustrated state forever behind, give him a sense of worth, cheer him up and to make the "impossible" person (because he had been "devouring") into what he really was: a serene young man, well on his way toward emotional maturity which would enable him to give his best on every level.

When we are obliged to cling to our blindness in this way, it is difficult to know how to interpret events, criticisms, for our unconscious helps us to dismiss them in order to justify ourselves.

If we do become intellectually aware of the

fact that we are taking ourselves seriously or playing a role—which is the same thing—and we desire to become authentic, that is, to integrate our self-knowledge with our lives, isn't it impossible on our own?

Despite our best efforts to understand our behavior in the light of this discovery on the intellectual plane, I must emphasize that we shall be incapable of full clarity, for it is on the emotional plane that our behavior is situated. Our unconscious, with its swift adjustments and acquired habits, is there to condition us and to prevent us from seeing clearly—in the real sense of the word. We are blind to ourselves.

Giving up our role is as difficult for us as for the mythological hero Nessus, who couldn't take off his tunic or he would die.

The assistance of others is indispensable if we are to discover the points at which our behavior does not "click" with the authenticity to which we aspire.

For that other, the role calls for the gentleness of a nurse treating a severe burn, as she gently removes with tweezers, bit by bit, the scraps of charred and dead skin. We must accept this aid, and that is possible only if we know that it is disinterested, completely objective, and motivated solely by a desire for our good.

We must be loved and love; know ourselves to be totally, unconditionally accepted; be sure that the discovery of this true personality which we are so jealously hiding, made at the price of a structure whose rigidity can make it seem impregnable (or so we hope and believe), will bring no harm to this acceptance, to this love.

Rosemary and Fred had taken Amy into their home. She had been in the grips of a severe depression and rejected by her family for various reasons which were associated with her behavior. Amy had a sense of security with this couple and was fully receptive to all the wise advice they gave her. Thus they were able to persuade her to move out of her apartment in order to save on rent, and they undertook all the details of the move, which would have been difficult in her state of health.

That done, Rosemary permitted herself, on several occasions, to make rather caustic and envious remarks about Amy's belongings. Amy, since she was single, could afford better things than could she, the mother of a family. Several poisonous comments on Amy's lingerie, her drapes, her dresses. . . . From that moment on, the bridges were down between her and Rosemary and Fred.

She accepted nothing more from them. Forced by circumstances—which they had largely created—to stay in their home, she closed herself to all advice, all help. She felt that they were no longer objective in relation to her, that they were reacting in terms of themselves and not of her. From then on she resented them out of the depths of her depression (which such an attitude is far form helping). Sunk under her guilt feelings, she henceforth regarded them as enemies. They could only destroy her.

This difficult undertaking of bringing assistance to others is possible only if it is motivated by true love and a mature and authentic friendship—that is, one which is unconditional and disinterested.

These poor people, who sometimes show so much self-assurance, are the most difficult to help. Doesn't that make it seem as if we might be wrong about them? And yet, if they do show so much self-assurance, if they also take themselves seriously and play a role, isn't it because they are profoundly unhappy? They did not receive, in their early childhood, the love which would have afforded them that self-confidence which would allow them to accept themselves as they are—that is, to recognize themselves as valuable—and therefore to be in harmony with themselves.

Most of the time, if not always, these are the frustrated people, and the frustrated are very difficult to help.

Actually, owing to their not being loved at the time when tenderness is the psychological key to growth, they are unable to believe in the love shown them. Unconsciously they cannot believe that they are loved. They feel that they are worthless. How could anyone love them?

They are demanding—it's something they can't help—always needing new (and exhausting) proofs of love when it has been given to them. At the same time they feel a "devouring" need to love, even more than to be loved. Indeed it seems to them such a miracle to be at last the subject of love for someone, to really exist for someone, that they are conscious of this truly "devouring" need to share everything, and thus to overwhelm, to spoil, to pamper the person loved, at the risk of smothering him and wearing him out.

We are all familiar with the cases of children who have been ill treated, and when someone has managed to establish a relation with them, to cross that defensive barrier they have set up between themselves and others, they show themselves as demanding, exclusive, literally clinging to the skirts of the instructor or the psychologist who knew how to find the way to their unhappy hearts and refusing to share her with anyone else.

It is the same way with adults. Consider again the case of John.

John was a very frustrated person whose mother had never known how to love him. Apparently self-assured, and with a brilliant intelligence developed by way of compensation for his maimed sensitivity, he was profoundly lacking in self-confidence underneath it all.

Marguerite's love revealed John to himself and gave him a little confidence in himself—he had at last been chosen, loved. Overwhelmed with joy, he became outgoing; he was able to take on responsibilities in his firm; he matured; and his friends, who thought he had found his salvation, were delighted.

But Marguerite, partly because she was tied

down by a narrowly conventional family who opposed this marriage for the sole reason that John did not belong to their social circle, and partly because she was made egotistical by serious personal problems, behaved in a very cowardly way. She felt suffocated by John's constant letters and phone calls and tried to tell him so; but since she didn't make the slightest effort to understand him, her protests were in vain: he was unable to modify his conduct.

She did not understand that this need of his was really "devouring," and that she could help him by showing him a patient and understanding love. She broke off their engagement three times for the most egotistical and trifling reasons— actually because he had caused her inconvenience and upset her family.

Each time, John hung on, explaining her attitude by her family's repressive influence and making excuses for her. In doing this, he based himself on what he believed to be proofs of her love for him. Actually it was herself and the love John had for her that Marguerite loved. She had never been capable of doing anything for him that involved trouble or inconvenience for herself.

She was fascinated by John's intelligence and flattered by his adoration of her. Isn't it delightful for a young woman to be worshipped in this way, the object of unnumbered attentions, each more delicate than the last? She never had any inkling of the degree to which her egotistical reactions, motivated on each occasion by anxiety for her personal comfort, were having repercussions on the emotional balance and the health of this young man whom she pretended to love.

Following each break-up John fell into a severe depression. He was able to lift himself out of it only by sheer courage, by persuading himself that he alone was to blame, that he didn't know how to love and had been wrong in doubting a love which was real.

Then he sought her out again, although she had not lifted a finger to help him during his time of misery. Flattered, she consented to these renewed meetings, happy to let herself be showered with gifts. Basically she was attracted to him. But once again, when he began to be a nuisance to her, she dropped him—"You're impossible! I can't do a thing for you."

But John, in his vital need to believe that he was still loved—in other words, accepted—tried to find excuses for her attitude. On one such occasion she had written to him in a letter just the night before: "Your love makes me bloom like a peony in the sun"; and he fastened onto these words, drawing sustenance from them in an effort to resuscitate the love he needed to believe in, in order to survive.

For three years, friends who knew them both were very clear on Marguerite's basic egotism and her cowardice. They tried everything in an effort to enlighten him and keep him from ruining himself for someone who was not worth the sacrifice. He had an answer for all their arguments (the unconscious is endowed with a formidable strength and skill in the preservation of our blindness): "I'm the only one who really knows her. Of course, she seems to be egotistical, but she does what she can. She is not sly, nor calculating, the way you say she is, nor cowardly. She's just a defenseless little girl. My love will save her from her wretched background."

Of course, it was a wretched background, but it was one to which Marguerite was attached by too many ties. Indeed, she was trapped; but, on the other hand, it was a life style to which she voluntarily adapted herself when it was to her advantage.

Friends were unable to help in this situation. What was needed was time and the Lord's intervention in putting true love on John's path, and with this gift, hope. Now his love met with a response and with understanding; he had the experience of certainty, and so he was able to take in the fact that for three years he had sustained himself on the illusion that he was loved.

Agnes saved him by loving him just as he was, by accepting him—insecurity, heaps of letters, and all; and the certainty that she was meant for him satisfied that devouring need of his, stilled the pangs of hunger which he had taken for love.

In two years she had transformed him into a calmer, more poised individual who had sufficient faith in her to make monopolizing her or suffocating her unnecessary; his love left her free.

Agnes' love made him into an adult on the emotional plane; he was capable of loving and being loved. Thanks to her, he turned over a new page in his frustrated life at the age of thirty, entering little by little, wonderingly, into that serene and peaceful kingdom to which only those have access whom someone has learned to love—and so has given a sense of worth and of security.

He was finally on the road to peace with himself. Very gradually, with the help Agnes gave him in seeing clearly, he was able to cast off the role he had been forced to play, and his excessive assurance and exhausting volubility along with it. He calmed down and developed a flexibility and resiliency which enabled him to absorb without any interruption of the peaceful rhythm of his life all those emotions which once would have had such severe repercussions on his equilibrium.

Unfortunately, it is not given to all who take themselves seriously to find on their path the rare individual who will love them with enough perseverance to help them free themselves from their yoke. But others can help us, when we are working with them as part of a team, to become aware of some of our relational difficulties and some of our incapacities. When this knowledge comes back to us through a group—as we have seen in the case of Claudia—it is often easier to accept. The entire technique of "group work" or psychological group study enables social workers, doctors, and other staff members, when they pool their experiences, to become aware of their difficulties in relating to patients, clients, or employees, and at the same time of the motivations which are their course.

And here we come to the help which specialists can bring us: from the social worker to whom we go to discuss the difficulties we are having with our adolescents or our old people to the psychoanalyst in the most serious cases; and, in between, the marriage counselor, the spiritual director, the psychologist, the psychotherapist.

Properly understood, the role of all these specialists is that of the mirror which reflects to us the image which we cannot see unaided. They are the catalytic agents whose listening presence, attentive silence, objective understanding, help us to become aware of the reasons which motivate our actions, and therefore to resolve our difficulties.

If they are able to give us valid assistance, isn't it because they have a disinterested love for us? Isn't it because their only object is our recovery, our maturation—seeing us reach the point at which we can sort out our own problems? They expect nothing for themselves.

Psychotherapy, psychoanalysis, social work— aren't they, in their true sense, a work of love? I think that all those who have had the good fortune to benefit by them can testify that this is so. It is love which is at work in the attentive listening, and in that confidence which is formed in relation to the possibilities of the one who is being helped, in whose ability to emerge from his state the helper believes.

And as for knowing how to be helped, wasn't this shown to us by the One who has said everything when, in his exhaustion, he said to the Samaritan woman, "Give me a drink"? He who was the Source of Living Water!

If God needs men, isn't it foolish pride and a total lack of realism to want to refuse the help they are ready to bring us?

Knowing how to learn from our failures

A failure, as we have seen, always has some lesson in it. We must develop both the knowledge and the ability to profit from our setbacks.

It isn't easy to do this on our own. A failure is always very frustrating—which is to say that it is traumatizing. And hence there is the danger that it will involve a hardening of the affectivity, which tends to armor itself a little more to protect itself both from suffering and from the reality which, often enough, it is not capable of facing.

The help of some outsider is needed to enable us to look at it squarely and to analyze its causes. This we cannot do unless it is dedramatized for us—that is, if someone helps us to reduce it to its real proportions, which are always relative, and put it in its place.

Shirley had just experienced a great failure: the end of a love affair. Since she was lacking in self-confidence she attributed the whole responsibility for it to herself in order to abase herself and prove to herself that she was incapable of loving, and therefore not an adult.

None of her friends, not even the doctor who attended her in the course of the severe depression which followed, helped her to put this failure in its place. Four months of total apathy had to pass before she discovered, by herself, that the responsibility for this failure was very much shared. Her partner in the affair had very neurotic emotional problems which forced him into attitudes which did not 'reflect his true personality. By being helped to become aware of this fact sooner, she could have been spared these months of severe illness. It would have been enough if someone had induced her to talk about her trouble and knew how to listen to her without judging her—because she "knew" this fact without being able to tell it to herself or see it.

When we take ourselves seriously, it is impossible for us to learn from our failures all by ourselves.

The self-serious tend to become isolated, quite alone, and refuse all help.

Is the problem insoluble? It could be hopeless for them—and for us, who can't help them. And the situation could become increasingly difficult since a badly assimilated failure is very traumatizing and can only bring on others.

What, then, can be done to help these frustrated people—that is, these people who have been deprived of love, so that they are constantly prevented form gaining confidence in themselves? How can one help them to learn from their failure?

It will call for much love, for that alone is

redeeming, and it really is a question of being redeemed. This means love as it is understood between man and woman, the love of friendship, and the patient and persevering love of comrades. Love has a thousand guises in which it shows itself; for us who are Christians, they are the thousand facets of Him who is nothing but Love.

When this love knows how to be patient and persevering in spite of the exhausting doubts and the devouring need for reassurance on the part of the person who lacks self-confidence, it will succeed in helping him. It will succeed in helping him to the extent that it compensates for the tenderness which was missing during his early childhood, the absence of which produced a hollow pit in the center of his sensitivity and affectivity which the years have only deepened and made more difficult to fill.

It is up to us who have been lucky enough to be loved, and to be able to love, to learn how to love unconditionally and with perseverance and understanding these people whose need for reassurance is so great; to enable them to attain their maturity, so that they will be able to love and be loved in their turn. To repeat, quoting now more fully, the passage from Claudel's *Le Perè humilié* which is like a refrain in this book:

While I am alone, says Pensée, I am someone who has no body at all, no position, no face. Only when someone comes . . . it is only then that I exist in a body. It is only through him that I know it.

This help from love permits the reconstruction of the personality, beginning with the affectivity. It gives the individual the ability to know himself, to accept himself; and in so doing it frees him for a spiritual evolution. He is, in fact, rigorously conditioned, and it is possible for emotional problems to paralyze him; that does not prevent the work of grace, to be sure, but it does make it more difficult.

As Claudel showed so well in his splendid drama *The Satin Slipper*, human love often opens the way to a more precise understanding of divine love. Often it is through human love, and thanks to it, that the person is able to burst the bonds of self, emerge from self, become conscious of the need to let himself be molded; and thus is achieved an integration, an interior harmony, which is far greater than what could be attained by the struggles of the will, which may be carried on for years without effect.

For the frustrated, the weak—those who are lacking in self-confidence—human love opens the way to patience and humility and leads them to prayer. It is then that through the vital center of their being, the superior part of the soul of which St. Francis de Sales speaks, the whole personality becomes serene, integrated; they learn to be still, in order to listen to the

sovereign melody of interior silence, which alone
is creative.

Knowing how to let events help us

Events are a veritable mine of lessons for
us—and not only those events which constitute
failures.

All social workers are familiar with those un-
stable workmen who go from job to job because
the foreman has it in for them—whereas the fact
of the matter is that they have not resolved their
problem with their fathers, whose authority
crushed them, and hence resent any manifestation of authority like three-year-olds terrorized
by parental abuse.

Then there is the fairly common type of the
insignificant-looking husband kept on a leash by
a virile woman; he often behaves like a tiger on
the job, if it involves a little authority. A man
like this is looking for weaker people than himself on whom to avenge himself and affirm
himself. All the aggressivity suppressed before
the Wife-Mother comes out in sadism practiced
on the "little guys."

These examples, presented somewhat at random, should suffice to suggest that the ex-
planation of situations and events is not always
on the surface, nor are events wholly fortuitous.

There are questions we might raise about our
own lives:

Why this series of accidents I've had on the

job? Is my job so unbearable that I unconsciously try to escape from it by letting it destroy me?

Why this accumulation of tickets for speeding? Does the lightness with which I take risks come from a dangerous overstimulation, excessive fatigue due to overwork, or what? Wouldn't it be a good idea for me to see a doctor?

Does the bad stretch I'm going through with the children have its origin in my attitude toward them, and does it call for a rethinking of the situation on my part, realistically and in all humility?

Does the loss of several important clients for reasons which seem entirely unrelated actually have its source in the way I am approaching them or treating them, or letting my employees treat them? Wouldn't it be wise to hold a staff meeting with a view to bringing to light the underlying reasons for the situation?

On the same line, is it possible that the serious personnel problems in the firm have their source in an attitude which is too remote or too authoritarian or unconsciously paternalistic?

Are we sufficiently aware of our class, regional, or ethnic prejudices? In rectifying this kind of blindness we have much to learn from the militant groups—black, chicano, even women's-lib.

Events have a way of being what we want them to be; what, in other words, we bring on—unconsciously, of course.

As for this matter of being led by our un-conscious, you may say: "It's stronger than I am"; or "There's nothing I can do about it"; or "I'm naturally hot-headed and impulsive, I have to be taken as I am; surely that's just life!"

Events often proceed from the attitude of others toward us, an attitude partly provoked by our own behavior. Don't we unconsciously ag-gress on them—all the more because we are lacking in self-confidence and take ourselves seriously?

In so doing, as we have seen, we are failing both in objectivity and in realism, the kind of realism which enables us to concentrate on events set in motion by others so that we can be flexible in adapting ourselves to them. We aren't alone on this earth, and we can't do anything without taking others into account; we can't realize our objectives or realize *ourselves.*

Claire presented herself to her new boss, who had manifested considerable skill and per-severance in obtaining her services from a de-partment which was unwilling to transfer her to him. In this way he had made his good will toward her very evident. In the course of the interview they had as she was starting off on the job, he explained that her duties would involve the distribution of relief. When she ventured to suggest, with great tact and prudence, that there were also educational aspects to the role of social service, he replied: "It will be four genera-tions from now before such an approach will be required of this service."

Claire understood that although the competence he had recognized in her had played a part in his asking for her, he was not prepared to accept her on the same footing as if she were a man. He had to demonstrate his aggressivity by deflecting her from her profession in order to assert himself as a boss and as a man.

Claire reacted to this insight by annihilating herself professionally for several months, taking care to prevent her educational experience from showing, and avoiding being referred to as a marriage counselor.

She had to get him to accept her as a distributor of relief before it was possible to establish a dialogue with him on another level. She "stuck to reality," a course in which she was assisted by failures she had had with earlier bosses from which she still smarted.

Doesn't the essence of Buddhism and the enlightenment it produces consist wholly in this: the desire for an interior change which will alter the attitude of others toward us and combat violence with nonviolence? It is a teaching which seems to be entirely individualistic; yet it involves an openness to others in this sense: that it is no less concerned with the establishment of peace and tolerance in our relationships with all those who are "not I." The effectiveness of my benevolent action toward my neighbor is conditioned by the quality of renunciation of myself.

Events are only what I allow them to make themselves.

When we stand back, so to speak, to review the course of our lives during the last ten or twenty years, doesn't the true meaning of our existence present a pattern as intricate as a filigree? And doesn't this pattern represent the dynamic relation between events and ourselves?

What a mistake it is to suppose that we can return to the past! If there is a sense in which life is an eternal return, it is also true that it moves upward in a spiral; each step discloses a new vista, but this means that we must keep climbing. Doors close behind us. The desire to alter this would be as vain as if we wanted to make the day last forever.

A poet-novelist, Paulette Houdyer, has remarked that scarcely has one paused in the ascent when already one is falling. Her phrase says it all.

When we have climbed high enough to gain perspective on our spiraling course, we must advert to the design, the rhythm, with a view to redressing the balance here and there—or to conform ourselves more closely to the pattern which has appeared, deriving comfort from it as well as instruction.

Yes, comfort; because very often the positive compensates for the negative, and in any case it enables us to limit the negative in the future.

But if we pause too long in the effort to let

light into this dense jungle which hides the edge of the forest from us, it will have the effect of a fall. It is a fall if we arrest our movement instead of allowing ourselves to be caught up in it. What is static is opposed to life—remember that the bicycle is upright only when it is rolling—and events constitute life in all the richness of its dynamism, its rhythm, its spiraling movement upwards toward that total fulfillment of our lives on the other side of that final birth which is death.

Learning to acquire humor

We have seen how lacking in humor people are when they take themselves seriously. They may have it with regard to other people all right, but never with regard to themselves. How could this be otherwise, since they are forced to play a role? Hence they are blind to themselves, *obliged*, in order to keep to the script, to see themselves only in terms of the role and in the reflection which others send back to them.

Once again, it is love which will help the frustrated person to stand off from himself sufficiently to see the funny side of his mishaps or of his eccentricities—something Molière and Montaigne, for instance, could do so well. Think of the use Molière was able to make of the treachery of Armande Béjart (from which he had suffered very keenly) and his painful struggles with the incompetence and the giddy ignorance of the doctors who finally succeed in killing him!

And Montaigne: think of the second book of *Essays* in which he describes his own appearance with a ferocious humor—his clumsiness, his lack of culture. It makes us wish we could acquire that kind of detachment from ourselves if we are able to recognize that we lack it.

There again, it is a question of accepting ourselves, and this acceptance enables us to find the reasons why we are as we are and to overcome them if need be, with the help of a marriage partner or a dear friend who is fortunate enough to have this precious faculty himself.

Their humor with regard to us in this situation is a refined form of charity, insofar as it enables us to stand off from ourselves, to de-dramatize even the severest trials and put them back into their (always relative) place.

There was Bertrand, age eighteen, the eighth in an impoverished aristocratic family. One day as he was setting out for Mass, his mother, looking him over from head to foot, said: "My dear, it would be interesting to know what is really your own in that rig. The trousers are your father's, the shirt is your cousin's, the vest is your brother's—whose, exactly, are the shoes?"

"But Mother," he replied, "the shoelaces are mine."

Humor permitted him to accept—with style—a

poverty which, at that point, was bordering on destitution.

How can we learn to acquire humor—or get it back, since we have noted that it is an innate sense in a child?

By analyzing it, of course; for what is it if not that clearheadedness which puts everything in its proper place—gives the great of the world only their real importance, removes so much of the sting from poverty and even death?

Why shouldn't this objectivity, this realism, be acquired? It calls for no more than forcing ourselves to stand back from ourselves (if we don't do it naturally)—from events and things, but ourselves first of all.

Who am I anyway, that so much importance should be attached to what happens to me?

Others before me have suffered from ill health, have lived in borrowed clothing. What does it matter to anyone but me, and why should others have to share the pain or the embarrassment such things cause me?

This is the first step.

The second step: Well, let us suppose ourselves faced with the death of a loved one. What is this atrocious suffering, this brutal uprooting of the dearest part of my being to leave a frightful void, in relation to the sufferings of the world?

Who am I to expect to be spared the fate which comes to so many others just as unhappy as I am? I unite myself to their suffering. I join my suffering to that of the Cross, and I stop talking about it and try to smile.

This effort to stand back from ourselves is very difficult to accomplish alone. Others help us a lot by their humor, that delicate flowering of charity of which Francis de Sales spoke as a connoisseur.

Those who are close to us, the events of life, and all those for whom being a humorist is a job—and a vocation—are there to teach us to acquire this attitude. It becomes a conditioned reflex, and as such it is the art of living. But there again, we must accept the fact that there are times in life when we are strong and times when we are weak. When something is hurting too much, or we are slowing down, unless we have kept this sense from childhood or developed it before this time, it would be like asking for the moon to hope for humor now.

On the other hand, let us profit by those times when things are more or less on an even keel, when we have our feet firmly on the ground, to subject ourselves deliberately to the discipline of looking at ourselves from the outside with as much of a sense of fun as we can muster. Believe me when I say that it helps. I know from experience.

There was Danios who took his severe nervous depression as the subject of his book and gave a dizzy account of himself, relating how he went from one city to another searching for "the" specialist who would understand him.

And there are Montaigne and Molière and so many others.

Couldn't we say, from their experience, that if humor is the refinement of charity it is also a strong factor of equilibrium?

[1] Marc Oraison, *Being Together: Our Relationships with Other People* (Garden City, N.Y., Doubleday, 1970), p. 133.

[2] *Ibid.*, p. 134.

[3] *Ibid.*, p. 137.

[4] Jacques Sarano, *Connaissance de soi, connaissance d'autre* (Paris, Centurion, 1967), p. 15.

[5] Sarano, *op. cit.*, p. 42.

[6] *Ibid.*, p. 78.

[7] *Ibid.*, p. 84.

[8] *Ibid.*, p. 94.

[9] *Loc. cit.*

[10] *Ibid.*, p. 36.

[11] *On Becoming a Person* (Boston, Houghton Mifflin, 1961), pp. 49-50.

Humor: Refinement of Charity and Factor of Equilibrium

Humor, refinement of charity

Isn't humor, to allude again to St. Francis de Sales' lovely phrase, the "delicate flowering of charity" which helps us to restore everything to its place (beginning with ourselves) within the framework of creation, society, and our own circle of associates?

Doesn't it help us to dedramatize the things that happen to us, the setbacks we experience?

A sense of humor is that natural awareness, intuitive but lucidly clear, of our own characteristic self among other persons—a deliberate look at ourselves which makes us smile. It is a perception which others help us to regain if we have lost it, or acquire if we have never had it.

It is a faculty we have for never believing that any event, good or bad, definitive, is "all over"; but at the same time it is something which helps us avoid getting "a swelled head" or falling into the nervous depression which awaits us if we take our own importance and the importance of our personal problems too seriously.

It is the sense of humor with which others regard us, but more particularly that with which we regard ourselves, which places us at the center of the real and of Reality itself.

There was Cecile, the mother of eight. She had very little help in coping with her family and might have been overwhelmed by work and fatigue. But she wasn't because she always saw the funny side of everything—not only external events but her own incompetence and absent-mindedness. And she did it before her children; that was important from their point of view:

"I didn't have time to go up and look at your rooms, boys. It must be quite a stable up there. And I don't dare think of the smell. If you are asphyxiated tonight, it will be just too bad about you . . . .

"Would you believe how half-witted I am? I've even missed the bargain sales. That means you'll have to offer me a new dress at the regular price, doesn't it, George? You'll love that, won't you, darling?"

There was Dorothy, who bravely made the best of a marriage which might have been a disaster by the humor with which she tried to look at both herself and David from the outside: "It has happened to others. Why make a big deal of it? Others besides me have managed to work things out."

Her good upbringing forbade her to put on an act about it and her faith gave her enough charity to find the merits—the five percent—in the poor boy (the victim of circumstances and especially of the destructive influence of his mother) whom she had been led into marrying.

There was Robert, who described his own clumsiness with riotous humor and told how he had broken some of the last of their best china while he was taking care of his bedridden wife.

There was Lucy, his wife, more than a semi-invalid. She sustained the morale of her neighbors by the droll humor with which she accepted everything, including her suffering, however intolerable it became.

We have already spoken of those for whom humor is a job and indeed a vocation. There is the clown, "that poet in greasepaint who puts self-satisfaction back in its proper place. He reminds man of his vulnerability; he denounces his folly. If all the miseries in the world fall down on him, it is so that he can catch them and annihilate them more easily. And when the tears come, the smile is not far away. The clown is always ready for a return match."[1]

Humor is gay, vivacious, malicious; the twinkle in the eye; the wink of complicity; the quick, sly look; the slight flare of the nostril which sometimes softens the irony of the lips.

The polite society of the seventeenth century

handed down humor to its descendants of the eighteenth, when the elegant practiced the art of consideration for others to perfection; they knew how to listen to the bores, to exchange subtle compliments; to engage in a raillery which was not wounding or tedious.

Isn't that the refinement of charity?

Nothing was serious in the eighteenth century, and that applies to the philosophers in particular; or rather, though they were serious, they did not wish to seem so. Taking yourself seriously was a manifestation of ill breeding.

Candide leaves us the pleasure of discovering the profound sense of the tale under all the banter—and what verve in the humor!

"It has been demonstrated," said Pangloss, "that things cannot be other than what they are; for having been made for one purpose, everything is necessarily for the best end." Even venereal disease!

My dear Candide! You remember Paquette, the maidservant of our august Baroness; in her arms I enjoyed the delights of Paradise which have produced the tortures of Hell by which you see I am devoured; she was infected and perhaps she is dead. Paquette received this present from a most learned monk, who had it from the source; for he received it from an old countess, who had it from a cavalry captain, who owed it to a marchioness, who derived it from a page, who had received it from a Jesuit, who, when a novice, had it in direct line from one of the companions of Christopher Columbus. . . .

O Pangloss, exclaimed Candide, this is a strange genealogy! Wasn't the devil at the root of it?

Not at all, replied that great man. It was something indispensable in this best of worlds, a necessary ingredient; for, if Columbus in an island of America had not caught this disease . . . we should not have chocolate and cochineal . . . .[2]

Talking about the value of lightness of heart, that very serious person J. Chateau writes in the no less serious *Revue philosophique:*

The non-serious can be mutual love, communication. The pleasantry is a social bond; it follows on the smile, the vestibule of humor. Sometimes a smile is meant to show that a person is not as serious as he seems to be. It is meant to soften criticism and produce a communion of minds which is foreign to the nature of the portentous man.

Sometimes a smile has the effect of turning our neighbor away from his preoccupation with selfish concerns and inviting him to a communion in the non-serious. Moreover, laughter cements the union of the people who are laughing; it has a social role if not (as Bergson thought) a social source. So does humor, that mixture of the serious and the non-serious.[3]

The humorist breaks the hold which the obvious has on us, because he is by vocation a nonconformist. And the change in lighting, so to speak, which results involves a transposition of reality like that of which the fable-maker who disguises men as animals is so fond.

A social role and the refinement of charity— don't they more or less amount to the same thing?

Humor, proof and factor of equilibrium

Because it is this natural awareness, intuitive and clearsighted—a smile directed at our characteristic self among other people—humor enables us to avoid taking ourselves seriously if it proves that we are not doing so.

I cannot laugh at my anguish unless I detach myself from it; unless I am capable—quite literally—of making fun of it.[4]

Robert Escarpit, a master of humor, has written a little book which is really the gospel on this subject.

Humor mitigates the destructiveness of irony by a wink of complicity. . . .

Humor possesses the virtues of humility and charity; they belong to the endowment of the humorists who help their fellow men to bear the minor troubles and the great agonies of the human condition. Between the lighthearted sketches of the cartoon to the sharp pen-strokes of the caricature which brings into merciless relief the grotesque detail, a whole gamut of nuances is expressed.[5]

Jean Duche, too, has much to teach us about humor, to which he refers somewhere as a Sister of Charity's gesture of love:

Hardly anything but sickness (sometimes) and death (always) justifies sadness. As for everything else—there is always something in it to laugh about. . . .
When we come to think of it, we realize that humor embraces sad things, and this is what made a wise man say that when we have stopped laughing it strikes us that we should have cried. But this wise man went on to observe that our having seized the laughable element is what brings healing.[6]

When we have a sense of humor we accept ourselves enough to be able to laugh at ourselves and what happens to us, and this is a kind of strength and a well-known source of poise:

Who is it that said that humorists are not haunted by the absurdity and cruelty of life, and so they don't try to vanquish the thought of these things by making believe that life is a game?[7]

The English are masters of the art of humor, but so too is Montaigne. Escarpit says that he is the first French man of letters to have manifested a really English sense of humor:
Let us open the second book of the *Essays*:

Now I am a little below medium height. This

is not only an ugly defect, but also a disadvantage ... for the authority given by a fine presence and bodily majesty is lacking. ...

Of music, either vocal, for which my voice is very inept, or instrumental, they never succeeded in teaching me anything: at dancing, tennis, wrestling, I have never been able to acquire any but very slight and ordinary ability; at swimming, fencing, vaulting, jumping, none at all. My hands are so clumsy that I cannot even write so I can read it. ... And I read hardly any better. I feel that I weigh upon my listeners. ...

My bodily qualities, in short, are very well matched with those of my soul. There is no liveliness. ... [8]

Humor is a discipline, and like every discipline it be learned. It is a discipline and an art of being, as Escarpit remarks in a pleasing passage:

Humor is an art of being—an art of being, not an art of living. It is neither dillettantism nor an intellectual panacea. [9]

There are many levels of existence, and that is why there are so many different kinds of humor which are so unlike each other. ... It is not to be identified with laughter.

If humor so often produces laughter, it is simply because its dialectic mechanism is analogous to that of laughter; it is because it readily, through the factor of irony, brings tension into being, and (though this is less often so than it used to be) on the rebound, when the tension breaks, leads to relaxation. It is possible for humor to coincide with the higher forms of dialectic thought and become philosophy. . . .

It is at once the will and the means of breaking out of the encirclement of automatisms which life in society—in short, life itself— crystallizes around us like swaddling bands, in a deadly kind of mothering.

Without humor men live the lives of larvae in their silken casing, sure of a brief future—half conscious, half unconscious, unchangeable.

Humor bursts the cocoon, opening it toward life, development, *the venture of being.*[10]

We recall the comparison we made between the butterfly leaving its chrysalis and the adolescent emerging into adult life. Isn't there a parallel here, since what is involved is a new openness toward that venture of being which is one of the characteristics of emotional maturity?

Emotional maturity is frequently demonstrated by men of considerable talent: we have already met Montaigne, Molière, Voltaire. Why should we not add those masters of life, the saints, whose wisdom is evident even to the eyes of the most worldly?

There was Monsieur Vincent. According to his own testimony he was "by nature of a bilious temperament and very subject to anger." But for divine grace, he says, he would have been "hard and repellent in temper, rough and crabbed." Instead, the observer was impressed by:

the discreet humor of the smile . . . around the

eyes, a thousand little wrinkles gave him a sunny look, a look which was that of intelligence, too, when intelligence gazes through goodness in order to see better.[11]

Monsieur Vincent, as we know, was chaplain of the galley slaves, and the story has come down to us of the occasion when, seeing a brutal overseer beating a slave too ill to work, he protested and asked that the man be sent to the hospital. The overseer agreed with the condition that Monsieur Vincent should take the man's place. Monsieur Vincent accepted, and he was found in this exercise by a servant of the galley general's wife who had been sent to look for him.

Frossard, in his report of the incident, comments:

. . . it fits in with the character of a hero who is always ready to take the Gospel literally and without gloss, and Gascon enough not to lose the chance of getting a fool into a scrape.[12]

Monsieur Vincent's exhortations to the community of nuns he founded have a touch of the poetic about them, a great intensity and—yes—humor, if it is the essence of humor to be at the heart of reality:

Your monastery will be the sickroom; your cell, a room you rent; your chapel, the parish church; your cloister, the city streets; your enclosure, obedience; your grille, the fear of God; your veil, holy modesty.

And there was St. Francis de Sales, the great bishop of Geneva, whose definition of humor as the "delicate flowering of charity" we have already quoted. He is famous, too, for his observation that one catches flies with honey, not vinegar. In his spiritual direction of so many married women in the world, he revealed a sensitive awareness of conjugal problems and of the realities of everyday life.

You must not only be devout, you must make devotion lovable.

This is what matters most: we must concern ourselves with what God wants; and when we have discovered it, we must try to do it gaily, or at least courageously.

Whatever kind of pickle God puts you in, it should be all the same to you. That is the stuff of the perfection to which we should all aspire.

Let us not sow our desires in our neighbor's garden but concern ourselves only with cultivating our own well.

What is the point of building castles in Spain when we have to live in France? This is an old axiom, and you know it well. Tell me, my daughter, do you practice it well?

To immodestly dressed widows he says, "If we don't want to receive guests, we should take down the 'Welcome' sign from the front of the house."

When the senate of Savoy threatened him with the unjust removal of his temporal power, he replied quietly:

The goods of the Church are like a beard; the more they are shaved, the thicker they grow; those who have nothing possess everything.

His whole period was won over by this sweet-natured humanism, and it comes to us like a ray of sunlight, still full of life and warmth, in the Salesian spirituality.

There was St. Thomas Aquinas, the Angelic Doctor. One day when he was lost in thought, one of his brethren called out to him: "Oh look! There is a flying ox!" To the immense entertainment of the community, he went to the window to look. On his return he retorted: "It would have been less unnatural to see an ox flying than a friar lying."

The great St. Theresa of Avila, from whose thoughts the Lord was never absent, frequently entered into dialogue with him—and in what a tone! One day when a heavy oxcart which was conveying her to one of her foundations had overturned in a stream, she complained to the One she called Your Majesty: "You have a very strange way of taking care of me! I almost drowned, and my nuns along with me!"

"That's how I treat my friends," he replied.

And she retorted: "I'm not surprised that you don't have more of them."

In that marvelous letter of hers to Philip II

she said very frankly, though with all respect due to the king, what she thought of his conquest of America and of the attitude of the clergy toward the poor Indians. No colonialist, and extraordinarily clearheaded, this Doctor of the Church!

It was Theresa, too, who, when the mystical raptures of a novice were described to her, counseled realistically: "Double her portion of meat and see to it that she eats it."

Theresa's realism amazes the psychologists. Thus she set down among the conditions of a good vocation that the young girl should not be subject to melancholy. "That kind of person," she said bluntly, "had better stay at home with her father."

She also said: "I am more afraid of a discontented religious than of a troop of demons."

We could go on endlessly passing in review all these individuals so well on the way toward emotional maturity—the definitive maturity of eternal life. Let us pause again on St. Therese of the Child Jesus. Popular imagery has distorted her thought and her spirituality, but the truth is that she in no way falls short of her great patron with respect to her solidity of personality, her great originality, and her courage.

There are external characteristics which we think of as affected; they are the fault of her style, which was the style of her time. But under all this what passionate ardor! What an iron will! Her abandonment of herself to God had nothing passive about it. To a novice who came to ask her advice, and finished off her recital with: "I see, Mother, that I have much to acquire," she retorted: "You mean to lose, my child."

Then there is Pope John, whose joyous spirituality had its wellsprings in the simplicity of his peasant good sense combined with a profound and transparent goodness.

We shall relate only two of the delightful anecdotes of which he was such an abundant source:

Receiving a superior general who introduced herself by saying: "Your Holiness, I am the Mother General of the Order of the Holy Spirit," he rejoined: "You are very lucky; I am only the poor Vicar of Christ."

Once, at an official dinner when he was Apostolic Nuncio in Paris, he was seated beside a woman in a remarkably low-cut dress. He was quite unembarrassed—he was far too well-balanced for that—but when it was time for dessert he chose for her, with great care, a beautiful apple from the fruit platter. "Why an apple, Your Eminence?" she said in a surprised voice when he offered it to her. "Madame," he replied, "it was when Eve had eaten the apple that she saw that she was naked."

We are not accustomed to think of the Scriptures as containing humor, perhaps because we confuse the sacred with the solemn. But let us consider, for example, the *Book of Proverbs*. It is, like so much of the Wisdom literature of the

Old Testament, almost violently misogynistic. That very fact, however, is in itself a source of humor. Archie Bunker is not funny to his "family"; he is to the T.V. reviewer, who sees in Archie's outrageous attitudes and actions a man who is humorous precisely because he has neither a sense of humor nor self-knowledge.

A continual dripping on a rainy day and a contentious woman are alike; to restrain her is to restrain the wind or to grasp oil in his right hand.

It is better to live in a corner of the housetop than in a house shared with a contentious woman.

Like a gold ring in a swine's snout is a beautiful woman without discretion. [13]

Analysts of humor have consistently pointed out that humor finds its source in the perception of incongruity, in the bringing together of ideas or realities usually thought opposed one to the other.

With this in mind, we can note the humor implicit in many of Our Lord's statements. We cite but several of the many readily apparent in the Gospels. Christ did not hesitate to use irony and even sarcasm, but these, too, are forms of the humorous:

Matthew 11:19 The Son of man came eating and drinking, and they say, "Behold, a glutton and a drunkard, a friend of tax collectors and sinners!" Yet wisdom is justified by her deeds.

Matthew 13:57 And they took offense at him. But Jesus said to them, "A prophet is not without honor except in his own country and in his own house."

Matthew 6:2-4 "Thus, when you give alms, sound no trumpet before you, as the hypocrites do in the synagogues and in the streets, that they may be praised by men. Truly, I say to you, they have their reward. But when you give them alms, do not let your left hand know what your right hand is doing, so that your alms may be in secret; and your Father who sees in secret will reward you."

Luke 7:24-27 When the messengers of John had gone, he began to speak to the crowds concerning John: "What did you go out into the wilderness to behold? A reed shaken by the wind? What then did you go out to see? A man clothed in soft raiment? Behold, those who are gorgeously appareled and live in luxury are in kings' courts. What then did you go out to see? A prophet? Yes, I tell you, and more than a prophet."

Luke 11:5-13 And he said to them, "Which of you who has a friend will go to him at midnight and say to him, 'Friend, lend me three loaves; for a friend of mine has arrived on a journey, and I have nothing to set before him; and he will answer from within, 'Do not bother me; the door is now shut, and my children are with me in bed; I cannot get up and give you anything'? I tell you, though he will not get up and give him anything because he is his friend, yet because of his importunity he will rise and give him whatever he needs. And I tell you, Ask, and it will be given you; seek, and you will find; knock, and it will be opened to you. For every one who asks receives and he who seeks finds, and to him who knocks it will be opened. What father among you, if his son asks for a fish, will instead of a fish give him a serpent; or if he asks for an egg, will give him a scorpion? If you then, who are evil, know how to give good gifts to your children, how much more will the heavenly Father give the Holy Spirit to those who ask him!"

Luke 18:2-7 He said, "In a certain city there was a judge who neither feared God nor regarded man; and there was a widow in that city who kept coming to him and saying, 'Vindicate me against my adversary.' For a while he refused; but afterward he said to himself, 'Though I neither fear God nor regard man, yet because this widow bothers me, I will vindicate her, or she will wear me out by her continual coming.'" And the Lord said, "Hear what the unrighteous judge says. And will not God vindicate his elect, who cry to him day and night? Will he delay long over them?"

John 18:20-23 Jesus answered him, "I have spoken openly to the world; I have always taught in synagogues and in the temple, where all Jews come together; I have said nothing secretly. Why do you ask me? Ask those who have heard me, what I said to them; they know what I said." When he had said this, one of the officers standing by struck Jesus with his hand, saying, "Is that how you answer the high priest?" Jesus answered him, "If I have spoken wrongly, bear witness to the wrong; but if I have spoken rightly, why do you strike me?"

Our Lord did not hesitate to use puns and near-puns—often derided as the lowest form of humor. It is noteworthy, however, that He uses them even in a context of utmost seriousness:

Mark 1:16-18 And passing along by the Sea of Galilee, he saw Simon and Andrew the brother of Simon casting a net in the sea; for they were fishermen. And Jesus said to them, "Follow me and I will make you become fishers of men." And immediately they left their nets and followed him.

Matthew 16:17-18 And Jesus answered him, "Blessed are you, Simon Bar-Jo'na! For flesh and blood has not revealed this to you, but my Father who is in heaven. And I will tell you, you are Peter, and on this rock I will build my church, and the powers of death shall not prevail against it."

It is difficult not to think of Our Lord smiling as he spoke, particularly in the case of "Peter," the name which Christ himself had given Simon when he called him—preparing for the pun he would later use when conferring the primacy on the man whose name meant, literally, "a rock."

It is equally difficult not to think of St. Luke smiling often as he chronicled in the Acts of the Apostles some of the bizarre adventures of St. Paul. Here, for example, is Paul imprisoned with his companion Silas at Philippi in Macedonia. They have been first beaten, then thrust into a cell with their feet in stocks:

Acts 16:25-40 But about midnight Paul and Silas were praying and singing hymns to God, and the prisoners were listening to them, and suddenly there was a great earthquake, so that the foundations of the prison were shaken; and immediately all the doors were opened and every one's fetters were unfastened. When the jailer woke and saw that the prison doors were open, he drew his sword and was about to kill himself, supposing that the prisoners had escaped. But Paul cried with a loud voice, "Do not harm yourself, for we are all here." And he called for lights and rushed in, and trembling with fear he fell down before Paul and Silas, and brought them out and said, "Men, what must I do to be saved?" And they said, "Believe in the Lord Jesus, and you will be saved, you and your household." And they spoke the word of the Lord to him and to all that were in his house. And he took them the same hour of the night and washed their wounds, and he was baptized at once, with all his family.

Then he brought them up into his house, and set food before them; and he rejoiced with all his household that he had believed in God.

But when it was day, the magistrates sent the police, saying, "Let those men go." And the jailer reported the words to Paul, saying, "The magistrates have sent to let you go; now therefore come out and go in peace." But Paul said to them, "They have beaten us publicly, uncondemned, men who are Roman citizens, and have thrown us into prison; and do they now cast us out secretly? No! let them come themselves and take us out." The police reported these words to the magistrates, and they were afraid when they heard that they were Roman citizens; so they came in and apologized to them. And they took them out and asked them to leave the city.

It would take a whole book to report the witticisms of St. Augustine. We are struck by the sparkle, the range, the "modernity" of his comments on subjects as universal as humanity itself. Wit abounds in his dissertations, his letters, his sermons, and his boldness is limited only by the bounds of his liberty—that is to say, his love.

He said of the Good Thief: "He stole everything, even heaven."

One doesn't have to yawn over St. Augustine's sermons. It was an eventuality he had anticipated. We read in his Teachings for the Catechumens:

The time comes when someone who gave us his willing attention at first, having wearied of listening or of standing up, ceases to praise us, and opening his mouth, begins to yawn, thus inadvertently demonstrating his desire to be gone. As soon as we have become aware of this, we must reawaken his attention by some discourse which, while it contains no impropriety, is a kind of light relief. Or, his mind should be presented with something startling, or pierced with some shaft which will move him to tears of sorrow and even concern him personally, so that his attention may be sustained out of self-interest. But let us be brief, since this is only a digression; otherwise, far from dispersing boredom, the remedy will only worsen the disease. Let us get on quickly with what we have to say, and let us promise, without fail, to be finished soon.

Without fail!

Then there is the prayer of St. Thomas More, so full of humor and so very English:

Give me a good digestion, Lord, and also something to digest.

Give me a spirit unacquainted with boredom, groans and sighs.

Don't let me worry too much about this encumbrance I call myself, Lord. Give me humor, so that I may extract some happiness out of this life, and let it be for the profit of others.

When More was mounting to the scaffold for his execution, the ladder leading to it was rickety. "I pray thee see me safe up," he said to the Lieutenant, "and for my coming down let me shift for myself." With his head on the block he made a delay to arrange his beard, saying that it was not to be cut since it had done no treason.

Another saint who suffered martyrdom: Joan of Arc. She was not intimidated by her judges—why should she have been, that girl who was above all free? "Don't all talk at once, noble Fathers," she said when they pressed her with questions.

Marie Gasquet describes her arrival at Troyes to the sound of bells and trumpets:

The clergy had come out to see Joan, a dazzling sight in her youth on her magnificent horse, the flapping of her banner in the breeze like the flight of doves. Anxious to assure themselves that it was a creature of flesh and bone they had before them, and not a diabolical apparition, they stood waiting at the gate with holy-water sprinkler upraised. "Come on, come on!" cried Joan, laughing. "I won't fly away"

Here she is again before her judges:

What form did Saint Michael have when he appeared to you?

I saw no crown on him; I didn't notice his clothing.

Was he naked?

Do you think Our Lord had nothing to clothe him with?

Did he have hair?

Why should he have cut it off?[14]

Closer to us in time is Bernadette, so full of childlike peasant wisdom. Once, having been asked to present a petition to the Blessed Virgin, she knelt down before a statute of St. Joseph. When her attention was called to this she said, "Sh! Don't say anything. They get along with each other in heaven." She was on familiar terms even with God.

Father Régamey goes a step further than Francis de Sales' definition of humor as the flowering of charity by suggesting that charity cannot exist here below when humor is wholly absent. We subscribe to this view, for there can be no charity except in humility; and when we speak of humility we are speaking of a clarity of vision, a sense of proportion, which is the essence of humor. All the saints we have touched upon thus far have abundantly demonstrated this to us. Perhaps it would be fitting to close this chapter with the Curé of Ars. We are so awed by his marvels of austerity that we are inclined to forget his humor, which was the product of total realism.

"Well-ordered charity," he said, "begins with

oneself. One must not exclude oneself from
one's own charity."

Once, having received two letters in the same
mail, he remarked:

In one they say that I am a great saint; in the
other, that I am a hypocrite and a charlatan. . . .
The first doesn't add anything to me, the second
does not take anything away from me. A person
is what he is in the sight of God, and nothing
more.

If, for all these saints in varying degrees, interior equilibrium expressed itself in terms of
joy and of wit as well, wasn't it because they
possessed that liberty which is the natural environment of the spirit and of the children of
God, according to St. Augustine's bold dictum:
"Love, and do as you will"? In their profound
realism, their active minds never lost contact with
reality.

The message of these Christian sages, of
whom St. Francis said, "They are to morals
what music performed is to the written score,"
is accessible to us all. Don't they confirm our
conviction that we mustn't take ourselves
seriously, that we must develop a sense of
humor? What this involves is being realists and
accepting ourselves in relation to others, and
even in relation to God.

Indeed for Christians being ourselves in relation to God means learning to lose many things,
as St. Therese of Lisieux has pointed out—that

is, to lose our petty ideas, our need for talk, in order to be still and listen to Him, letting Him, the Infinite, invade the narrow, limited, finite humanity which is ours as creatures whom He has nevertheless created to share one day the glory and the totality of His own life.

[1] Jean Monteaux, *Célébration du cirque* (Paris, Robert Morel, 1965), p. 34.

[2] Voltaire, *Candide* (New York, Modern Library), p. 117.

[3] "Le sérieux et son contraire," *Revue philosophique*, October-December 1950, p. 456.

[4] *Ibid.*, p. 449.

[5] Robert Escarpit, *L'humour*, P.U.F., Collect. "Que sais-je?" (Paris, 1955), p. 44.

[6] Jean Duche, *On s'aimera toute la vie*, pp. 140-141.

[7] Escarpit, *op. cit.*, p. 83.

[8] Stanford, California; Stanford University Press, 1958, pp. 485-487.

[9] *Op. cit.*, p. 127.

[10] *Loc. cit.* (italics mine).

[11] A. Frossard, *Votre très humble serviteur St. Vincent de Paul* (Paris, Bloud et Gay, 1960), p. 20.

[12] *Ibid.*, p. 112.

[13] This and the other excerpts from Scripture which follow are from *The Holy Bible: Revised Standard Version* (New York, Nelson, 1953). Copyright 1946 and 1952 by the Division of Christian Education of the National Council of the Churches of Christ in the U.S.A. and used by permission.

[14] Jules Jacques and Kerwyn Ten Driessche, *L'humour chez les Saints* (Paris, Bloud and Gay, 1938), p. 157.

Conclusion

The danger of being serious—isn't this a question which concerns us all? Don't we all take ourselves a little seriously in some area or other? As parents, bosses, social workers, teachers or whatever? No one escapes it entirely, for as we have seen, very few attain to the complete fulfillment of their emotional maturity here below.

It is no longer possible to divide humanity into two parts, the normal individuals and those who are ill. . . . There are those who experience insurmountable difficulties in certain sectors of their personality owing to present effects of conflicts insufficiently resolved.

A certain number of these people, in various ways, decide to ask for help from someone. This can take a variety of forms, ranging from what is called "spiritual help" through recourse to a doctor, all the way to psychotherapy as such and—at the extreme—psychoanalysis. There is no "frontier," with you and me on one side and the gravely ill mental patient on the other.[1]

We all have, at every age, the possibility, if we will consent to it, of getting to know ourselves better so that we can accept ourselves a little more, and setting out from this dynamic knowledge, improving ourselves a little at a time. This will be all the easier if we will let ourselves be helped by other people, by events, and by life.

We have only to remind ourselves of that five percent of good which exists in the worst criminals—surely there is more good in us than that? Then, however frustrated we have been with regard to love in our early childhood, we shall be able to love ourselves just a little— enough, perhaps, to accept the idea that others can love us, and hence help us. They will enable us to acquire that dynamic, accepting self-knowledge which is on the way to something better, and consequently the source of courage and optimism.

But time and patience are needed—and as Talleyrand put it, "Not too much zeal!"

There is a knowledge of self and of others which is not acquired by dint of effort, nor the tortured searching of the intelligence; it is a matter of another kind of intelligence defined as "discernment"—what St. Therese called "understanding." It consists in receptiveness rather than activity, in humility and humor; in yielding more than in doing. We ourselves don't matter very much in this; it is something accomplished in us.

This knowledge is not something we possess; rather, we belong to it, it possesses us. Yet it enables us really to regain possession of ourselves and of those we love, not by way of acquisition but through receptiveness, through listening and through abandonment.[2]

It means avoiding too much zeal, learning to be patient with ourselves, available to ourselves, to others and to life. It means being sufficiently relaxed in the depths of our being to allow ourselves to be helped, gently, by everything in our environment, to be sustained by the humble solidity of things. The yielding of grass to the wind; the gaze of a child, even when his candor catches us off guard; listening in silence to someone who is poorer than ourselves, and enduring greater trials; the joyous trilling of a bird; the fraternal correction of a comrade; the counsel of a friend; above all, the love of one who loves us for better and for worse: all these things sustain us.

It will mean learning—at first intellectually but then, above all, affectively—to extract the positive value from everything, letting ourselves be impregnated by it like an open field in which the new seed ripens. It will mean learning to let it work in us without resistance, absorbing it the way a porous surface drinks in the moisture in the atmosphere, the way the earth gently absorbs the rain which makes it fertile in its depths.

We can improve ourselves if we love ourselves enough to accept being loved and helped by others; if we love ourselves enough to believe that love is all-powerful and to consent to open ourselves up to its creative action.

Can a work of this kind have any other aim than to show each individual the possibilities he has for improving himself? These possibilities always lie open to us because they have their source in the capital of Love on which they are established—the Love with which creation over-flows but which the world denies because it does not know how to see Him. But we Christians believe in it as we do in the reality of our existence.

[1] Oraison, *op. cit.*, p. 136.
[2] Sarano, *op. cit.*, p. 203.